HAWKER HURRICANE

Inside and Out

Melvyn Hiscock

The Crowood Press

First published in 2003 by
The Crowood Press Ltd
Ramsbury, Marlborough
Wiltshire, SN8 2HR

www.crowood.com

Text © The Crowood Press Ltd 2003
Illustrations © Melvyn Hiscock 2003, except where otherwise credited

British Library Cataloguing-in-Publication Data
A catalogue record for this book is available from the British Library.

ISBN 1 86126 630 8

Acknowledgements
This book would not have been possible without the generous assistance
of Tony Ditheridge of Hawker Restorations, who has allowed full access
to his company over several years. Steve Vizard of Airframe Assemblies
provided full access to his factory, where several sets of wings have been
made. Chris Michell, also of Airframe Assemblies, provided photographs
of the wing build process and the Mark I wing. Lewis Deal allowed full
access to the Hurricane on display in the Spitfire and Hurricane
Memorial at Manston. All of these people have been generous with their
time and expertise.

PREVIOUS PAGE: Hurricane XII G-HURI taking off from a charity fly-in at
the small private strip at Old Hay, Kent, in July 2002.

Typeset by NBS Publications, Basingstoke, Hampshire

Printed and bound in Malaysia by Times Offset (M) Sdn Bhd

Contents

Introduction

OVER the past ten years or so, the Hawker Hurricane has managed to regain its place in history. For too long, the Supermarine Spitfire was given the greater credit for winning the Battle of Britain, while the Hurricane was overlooked, despite having been available in greater numbers and scoring more victories. This was due at least in part to the publicity that the Spitfire received at the time, and to the general public's perception of events as gleaned from newspapers. With the benefit of hindsight and good methodical research, the Hurricane's place as a truly historic aircraft is now well established. However, there are still misconceptions abounding about the aeroplane, what it was capable of and how it was built.

The Hurricane was designed at a time when enormous changes were taking place in aviation. Throughout the 1920s and 1930s, fighter aircraft had changed relatively little from the machines seen in World War I. They were still biplanes with fixed undercarriages and armed with rifle-calibre machine guns. Fighters up to and including the Hawker Fury and Gloster Gauntlet were armed with two Vickers machine guns, exactly as the Sopwith Camel had been in 1916. By 1930, the speeds of bombers in service, such as the Fairey Fox, had increased to the point where fighters struggled to catch them and engagements were fleeting. The lack of hitting power inherent in only two machine guns became a problem, as there was simply insufficient time to deal a killing blow in a short burst.

In response to this problem, fighters were made faster and equipped with more guns. However, the extra guns created more weight, and so more powerful engines were required just to keep the performance of the fighters equal to those that had gone before. Several of the engines then in service, such as the Bristol Jupiter, were also beginning to reach the end of their development potential.

In 1930 the Air Ministry issued Specification F7/30, calling for a day and night fighter with a top speed of 250mph (402km/h) and four machine guns. The winner was the Gloster Gladiator, which entered service in 1937. This was the first RAF fighter to have an enclosed cockpit and wing flaps.

In April 1935, the Bristol Aeroplane Company flew its Type 142, a fast twin-engined monoplane transport aircraft with retractable undercarriage, which had been ordered by the newspaper tycoon Lord Rothermere. With a top speed of 307mph (494km/h),

it was some 50mph (80km/h) faster than the Gloster Gladiator, which, at that point, had still to enter service. It was a relatively simple matter for Bristol to redesign the Type 142 as a medium bomber, and so the Bristol Blenheim was born. It was clear that the days of biplane fighters, with their inherent drag disadvantage, were numbered, and that even four machine guns were not going to be an adequate armament for the next generation of fighters.

Speed and Firepower

Several of the F7/30 contenders had been powered by the Rolls-Royce Goshawk engine, a development of the excellent 23.5ltr V-12 Kestrel engine. The V-12 featured evaporative cooling, which required steam condensers that generally formed part of the aircraft's skin. Among these contenders had been R.J. Mitchell's Type 224, his fixed undercarriage monoplane fighter project that gave no clues as to just how good the Spitfire would eventually become.

Hawker's proposal for the F7/30 specification was a development of the Fury known as the PV3, with PV standing for private venture. This was an enlarged development of the Fury then in service with the RAF, and was initially powered by a Rolls-Royce Goshawk III engine. The steam condensers for the engine cooling were an integral part of the upper wing structure. As well as being larger than the Fury, the PV3 also had a swept-back upper wing similar to that fitted to the Hart series, in order to maintain the centre of gravity with the heavier Goshawk engine. The four machine guns were installed in the fuselage, with two in front of the pilot and two along the sides of the fuselage close to the pilot's legs. In both cases, the breeches could be accessed to clear any of the stoppages that were a fact of life with the guns of the period.

The PV3 flew with the Goshawk III on 15 June 1934, but in June 1935 a new engine, a Goshawk B41 of 700hp, was installed. With this, the PV3 had a top speed of just 224mph (360km/h) and could climb to 20,000ft (6,100m) in slightly over twelve minutes. These figures were similar to the Fury II, and so the only advantage of the PV3 over the Fury was two extra guns, although these had less ammunition per gun. Clearly there was still a long way to go.

Tests carried out during 1934 at Martlesham Heath in Suffolk, the Air Ministry's centre for flight-testing RAF and civilian aircraft, had shown that eight .303 guns firing at 1,000 rounds per minute would be required to ensure the destruction of a target in a short burst. As a result of these findings, Specification F5/34 was issued, calling for an eight-gun fighter that was capable of 275mph (443km/h).

This air-to-air view of a Hart was originally published in *Flight* in June 1930. Many of the features are very similar to the Hurricane. (*Aeroplane Monthly*)

However, both Hawker and Supermarine had been working independently to improve their designs that had been rejected in the Specification F7/30 competition. Chief designers R.J. Mitchell at Supermarine and Sydney Camm at Hawker could both see that the future lay with advanced monoplanes, and so had been working to refine their designs for greater performance. By 1933, Sydney Camm had drawn a monoplane Fury, but its performance was limited by the Goshawk engine and his decision to use a fixed undercarriage.

In January 1933, Rolls-Royce started work on its private venture engine, the PV12. This first ran in October the same year, and by July 1934 had passed its 100-hour type test, rated at 635hp for take-off and 790hp at 12,000ft (3,650m). It clearly had tremendous development potential, and by December 1935, when it passed its fifty-hour civil type test, it was producing 955hp at 11,000ft (3,350m). By now, it had become known as the Rolls-Royce Merlin, an engine that many still believe to be the finest piston aero engine ever produced.

The new engine was exactly what Camm and Mitchell required. Mitchell went on to design the Spitfire and Camm enlarged his Fury monoplane design as the Hawker High Speed Interceptor. The Air Ministry was impressed enough to order one pro-

totype, issuing the Specification F36/34 for the purpose. It also ordered one prototype aircraft from Supermarine under the Specification F37/34. The Hurricane and the Spitfire were born.

The potential of these new designs was such that they effectively superseded the earlier Specification F5/34. However, those designs already started were continued as insurance should either the Spitfire or Hurricane fail.

The F5/34 included the Vickers Venom, a development of the earlier Vickers Jockey, a contender for Specification F20/27 that had led to the Gloster Gauntlet. Powered by the 625hp Bristol Aquilla engine, the Venom managed 312mph (502km/h) at 15,000ft (4,570m) and was very manoeuvrable. However, the Aquilla engine was not considered to be a major production engine and no other engine of similar power and diameter was available. The 890hp Bristol Perseus would have given much improved performance, but was too wide to fit the fuselage.

The Bristol Aeroplane Company had produced two contenders for the earlier F7/30 specification, and the experience gained from this process was incorporated into the Type 146 for Specification F5/34. The Type 146 was a low-wing, all-metal monoplane designed around the 835hp Bristol Perseus radial. This engine was not ready for the prototype, which

The Hawker Fury has often been described as the most beautful biplane ever built; this is the navalized version, the Nimrod.

instead flew with a Bristol Mercury. Delays in building the prototype and its disappointing performance, a top speed of 287mph (397km/h) at 15,000ft (4,570m), did not help the project. It was damaged in a landing accident at the 1938 Empire Air Display at Filton, when it collided with a structure built for the display finale, and as a result the Type 146 was scrapped.

At the Gloster company, chief designer H.P. Folland had originally planned a monoplane version of the Gladiator, but this developed into an all-metal, low-wing monoplane powered by the 840hp Bristol Mercury IX engine. This gave it a top speed of 316mph (508km/h) at 16,000ft (4,880m), which was as fast as the Hurricane prototype. However, the Mercury engine was at the end of its development, although fitting the higher-powered Bristol Taurus would have been possible. The Gloster F5/34 had considerable design potential and excellent flying characteristics, but did not proceed due to the success of Mitchell's and Camm's designs.

Construction

Many accounts of the rearmament programme in the late 1930s refer to the complexity of the Spitfire compared with the simplicity of construction of the Hurricane. It is also said that the Hurricane has a direct lineage from the 'stick and string' biplanes of

World War I. Whilst this may appear correct on the surface, in truth it is far from being the case. The Spitfire is a monocoque structure that is relatively easy to make once the relevant skills have been acquired, whilst the Hurricane was built around a steel tube frame, faired with wood and fabric. Even this does not adequately describe the complexity of the Hurricane structure, as will become apparent in the following pages.

The Hawker company had grown from the remnants of the old Sopwith company, after Sopwith had gone into liquidation following the cancellation of contracts after World War I. Sopwith aircraft had all been produced with a conventional wooden structure of spruce spars and plywood ribs in the wings, with ash or spruce longerons and spruce crosspieces braced with piano wire in the fuselage. Sopwith was better organized than some manufacturers, in that it used standard fuselage fittings across the range of aircraft built during the war. The fuselage fittings, which connected the various components and to which the cross-bracing wires were also fitted, were therefore the same on the Sopwith Snipe of 1918 as they had been on the Sopwith Tabloid of 1914.

Early Hawker aircraft were built the same way, but gradually metal replaced the wooden parts, partly due to weight and strength considerations and partly due to ease of material supply, metal being far more consistent than wood. This was a process that evolved, and in doing so became quite complicated. However, it was helped by economy of scale, since many of the same processes were used across the range of aircraft built by Hawker, and in some cases by Gloster, which had been bought by Sopwith in 1934 as the basis of the Hawker Siddeley Group.

The all-metal structure had been evolved by Fred Sigrist in the early 1920s and had first been used on the one-off private venture Hawker Hornbill fighter of 1925. Rather than use welded joins between tubes, as had been pioneered by Fokker in World War I, Sigrist developed a system where the fuselage tubes were rolled to a square section at their ends. These were then joined by stainless steel plates riveted or bolted to the tubes. The bolts passed through spacers within the tube to prevent it from being crushed. The frame was then cross-braced with wires in the same way as wooden fuselages had been. The wing spars were also developed at this time. They consisted of two twelve-sided booms that were rolled from flat high-tensile steel plate. These had flanges on to which the web, which kept the two booms of the spar apart, could be riveted; again, they were more complicated than initial inspection might suggest. The patent for the wing spars was in the name of Roy Chaplin, who had joined Hawker in 1926 as Sydney Camm's assistant.

The classic lines that evolved into the Hurricane were first seen on the Hart series of bombers and fighters, which were arguably the most attractive weapons ever built. They dispensed with earlier radial engines and were fitted with the Rolls-Royce Kestrel V-12, which gave more appealing cowling lines. The Hawker Hart had, in fact, been one of the early bombers whose development had caused a stir in fighter design, as it was faster than contemporary RAF interceptors. This led to a fighter variant, the Hawker Demon, and the type was developed into the Hind day bomber, which saw service in the Middle East, and into the Hector, an army co-operation aeroplane. The Hart series also had some export success.

The prototype Hurricane was built in much the same way as the earlier biplanes, except for the ribs being made of metal rather than wood. The wing was built in three parts: a constant chord centre section housing the undercarriage; wing fuel tanks and oil tank; and outer wing panels. On the prototype these differed from the production versions as they had no sweepback on the leading edge, allowing a straight front spar. The wings utilized the Warren girder principle, which uses the inherent strength of the triangle. The compression members, which hold the spars apart on

the wing, were angled to form triangular sections within the wing. This made for a very strong but light structure that withstood the bending and drag loads and had a high degree of torsional stiffness.

The loads produced by aileron deflection at high speeds can cause the rest of the wing to flex, with the aileron acting on the wing in the same way that a spring tab would act on an aileron. This can produce an opposite effect to that required, or indeed expected, by the poor pilot, as the wing achieves a greater or lesser angle of attack as it is forced to bend by the aileron. In extreme cases, where wings have insufficient torsional strength, this can lead to complete loss of control, which, of course, can result in overstressing and structural failure.

Biplane wings are much less prone to this problem, as the bracing between the pairs of wings helps to maintain the structural integrity. Also, their relatively low speeds do not impose the same loads.

The covering of the wings was not as it had been on most biplanes. These had the fabric stitched to the wing with waxed string, as had been done since before World War I. The Hurricane, with its higher speed, would have suffered from the extra drag of the stitching and so a new method was employed. The boom of the wing rib, the piece that made the airfoil section running fore and aft, was made as a channel. The fabric was let into this and another channel piece was clamped down on top to hold the fabric into place using bolts with captive nuts. The channel was then covered by fabric tape, making a much smoother wing.

The fuselage frame was faired with wooden formers and longitudinal stringers to give the outer shape before being covered in fabric. The area around the cockpit was built from formers and skinned in plywood and is generally known as the 'doghouse'.

One feature of the Hurricane that was well liked by ground crews was the number of removable panels on the side of the fuselage that gave excellent access to the engine, fuselage area and cooling system All of these panels were attached by Dzus fasteners to a metal frame, fixed to the load-bearing structure of the fuselage. The fuselage was bolted to the centre section of the wing at four pick-up points that attached to the front and rear spars.

The cockpit was fully enclosed with a sliding hood, which, on the prototype, had only a single vertical frame member between the front and rear frames. For the early tests, no gunsight or armoured glass was fitted to the cockpit. The cockpit was entered from the port side, where there was a retractable step built into the bottom of the fuselage. Pulling this out also opened a spring-loaded handhold by the cockpit.

The Hurricane prototype at Brooklands in its first flight configuration. Note the strut-braced tailplane, the short radiator housing and the lower undercarriage doors. (*Aeroplane Monthly*)

The undercarriage retracted inwards and slightly backwards, using an ingenious cam system to clear the front spar. As a result, the Hurricane had a wide track of 7ft 7in (230cm), which made it relatively easy to handle on the ground. The wheels were also totally enclosed when retracted. The undercarriage legs carried the doors, the bottom part of which was hinged to swing outwards when the gear was lowered to clear the ground. Operation of the undercarriage and flaps was hydraulic.

The tailplane on the prototype was designed and stressed as a cantilever structure, but was strut-braced to the bottom longeron in case the tail showed any signs of flutter during test flights. These were removed during the tests as flutter was not found to be a problem.

The rudder had no horn balance, as on the production versions, but a balance weight that protruded from the top of the rudder. The tailwheel on the prototype was, like the main undercarriage, retractable.

The fuselage was built up in the standard Hawker fashion, the sides forming another Warren truss. Initially, the prototype was made to be fitted with two guns either side of the cockpit and two in the wings, as in Specification F7/30. This was changed to the eight-gun armament before the first flight, although there are photographs of the prototype fuselage with machine guns fitted to the sides.

Gun Development

Many of the twin-gun fighters of World War I and the interwar period used the Vickers gun. This was an air-cooled development of the water-cooled infantry gun. These were, by 1939, old technology (although they

remained in service for most of the war) and were prone to jam. This was not too much of a problem if the breeches were close to the pilot, as he could (if not too busy avoiding being shot down) clear the jam. However, this would have been impossible if the gun was in the wing.

The Air Ministry decision to adopt the Browning machine gun as the standard was made during 1934. Trials were held and a variety of rifle-calibre guns were tested. These included the Mark 5 Vickers gun and the Colt .300. Larger calibre guns, the .5in from Colt and the 20mm Hispano cannon, were also tried at this time, but were rejected as being too bulky, slow firing and unreliable.

The Colt .300 was a development of another World War I infantry gun, which had been designed by John Browning, and which had been completely redesigned in 1933 to provide an air-cooled gun for use in aircraft and on tanks. The Colt was far superior to all other guns tested in terms of rate of fire and reliability and so a licence was bought to produce the gun in the UK with the bore increased to .303 to fit the standard ammunition, and renamed the Browning.

Engine

The engine on the prototype was a pre-production Merlin C, serial number 11, turning a Watts two-bladed, fixed-pitch wooden propeller. It was with this engine combination, on 6 November 1935, that Hawker test pilot P.W.S. 'George' Bulman took the High Speed Interceptor for its maiden flight. The first flight was a gentle affair as the engine was still under development and had not yet passed its 50-hour type test. Since the objective was to test the whether the

Early engine running on the prototype. There is no known photograph of the first flight, but this would have been taken at around the same time. (*Aeroplane Monthly*)

controls worked as designed and the aeroplane actually flew, Bulman did the entire flight with the undercarriage locked down. Airborne retraction tests could be carried out later.

Further flights followed until 26 December, when the engine was changed for Merlin C no.15. The early Merlins were suffering from the inevitable teething problems of a new engine and the Merlin had yet to achieve its legendary reliability. This left the prototype grounded until February when the new fighter was prepared for its Service testing at Martlesham Heath, being delivered there on 28 February 1936. At this point, the aeroplane was ballasted with the equivalent weight of four machine guns.

The Martlesham pilots found the fighter to be simple to fly, but the controls proved heavy at high speed. They also said that the stall was viceless and they found the top speed to be 315mph (507km/h) at 16,500ft (5,030m). The fighter clearly had a future, and so the Hawker board took the somewhat risky step of tooling up for production of 1,000 aircraft before an order had been received. The board was rewarded on 27 June 1936 when the Air Ministry ordered 600 aircraft, a massive order by the standards of the time. Approval was given to use the chosen name for the new fighter, which from then on became known as the Hawker Hurricane.

During the testing of the prototype, the lower folding gear doors were removed. It was felt that the small increase in top speed that these gave was not worth the maintenance effort of things that would spend most of their time on the ground in close proximity to mud.

In early tests, the canopy had given some cause for concern, as it was seen to flex at speed. This resolved itself, fortunately without injury to the pilot, when it flexed enough to detach itself in flight and was lost. A sturdier canopy with additional framing was fitted in its place. It was at about this time that the tailplane strut was also removed, having been found to be unnecessary.

During August 1936, the prototype was fitted with the eight-gun armament in a second pair of wings. There was a slight change to the internal structure of the wing to enable the guns and ammunition chutes to be fitted between the diagonal wing structure. The lightening holes in the diagonal members were rearranged to allow equipment to be fed into place, and the guns were staggered so that the ammunition feeds and shell ejectors did not foul. A ring and bead sight was also fitted at this time.

Another modification was to the starboard side of the cockpit, where a push-out panel was included to make exit from the Hurricane easier in an emergency when wearing full military kit.

The troublesome Merlin C, of which a total of four were fitted to the prototype through its testing, was developed into the Merlin F, which became the production Merlin I. The production Hurricane was designed around this, but Rolls-Royce produced an improved version, the Merlin II, which was put into production after just 180 Merlin Is had been built.

The prototype at a later stage in its flight-testing. Here it has lost the tailplane strut and has the replacement canopy, fitted after the first was lost. Also of interest is the starting handle for the starter magneto. (*Aeroplane Monthly*)

The prototype in flight. It has the later canopy, unbraced tailplane and is yet to have its armed wings fitted. (*Aeroplane Monthly*)

The change gave an increase in power and reliability but necessitated a redesign of the cowling lines, which held up the production Hurricane by five months.

The Production Hurricane

The first production Hurricane, L1547, was test-flown by Philip Lucas on 12 October 1937. Within a week, it was followed by the second. By the end of November 1937, seven production Hurricanes had been manufactured. By Christmas 1937 testing had gone well enough to allow No. 111 (Fighter) Squadron to equip one flight of four aircraft; by February, the squadron was fully equipped. The production Hurricane was capable of 316mph (508km/h), similar to the prototype but with the added weight of military equipment.

The production Hurricane differed from the prototype in several ways. The most obvious was that the wing gained a moderate sweep with the front spar angled backwards slightly. This was due to the additional military equipment moving the centre of gravity backwards. The flaps, which on the prototype were fitted across the whole of the centre section, were now spilt, as a redesigned radiator housing had taken up some of the space. The slight decrease in flap area did not adversely affect the handling.

The hood had been redesigned and was stronger but had slightly less glass than before, which somewhat impeded the pilot's view. A standard blind-flying panel had been fitted in the cockpit in common with all RAF aircraft of the period.

Early production Mark I Hurricanes still featured the retractable tailwheel and two-bladed fixed-pitch propeller, and the wings were still fabric-covered. However, it was in one of these that Commanding Officer of 111 Squadron, Squadron Leader J. W. Gillan, made sensational news. On 10 February 1938 he flew to RAF Turnhouse, near Edinburgh in Scotland. The flight to Turnhouse had been made against strong headwinds but on the return these helped Gillan average 408.7mph (657.8km/h) over the 327 miles (526km) back to Northolt. This feat was heavily publicized by the RAF, leaving the public in no doubt that the RAF had a formidable new fighter.

Gillan also worked hard to dispel some of the myths that had grown up around the new fighter and trained his squadron pilots to get maximum performance from the aircraft. Because it was so much faster than previous aircraft but still very manoeuvrable, pilots were subjected to higher 'G' forces. They also had to deal with an aircraft that was certainly more complex than what they had been used to. Accidents did happen, but

The differences between the prototype and the early production Hurricanes are visible on this view of L1582. This has the two-bladed Watts propeller, the early type of air intake, ring and bead sight, fabric-covered wings and straight aerial. It has yet to be fitted with the ventral fin and rudder extension. This Hurricane eventually went to No. 3 Squadron and then to 73 Squadron at Digby, where it crashed on 4 August 1939. (*Aeroplane Monthly*)

L1791 shows the de Havilland two-pitch propeller but this Hurricane still has fabric-covered wings, ring and bead sight and the early radio mast. (*Aeroplane Monthly*)

as experience with the new type increased and training continued, these lessened.

The first changes to appear on the production Hurricanes were the addition of an anti-spin strake below the rear fuselage, in front of the tailwheel, and the addition of a fixed, instead of retractable, tailwheel. Spinning trials on the prototype had shown a marked reluctance for it to come out of the spin. In his first spin, Philip Lucas started at 18,000ft (5,490m) and only recovered at 2,000ft (610m), which was far too low for comfort. The Hurricane tended to develop a slow, stable and fairly flat spin, and the elevators were not effective enough to give sufficient movement for the plane to break out of the spin. The answer came in providing the anti-spin strake beneath the fuselage and extending the rudder downwards to line up. This also helped lateral control in the landing configuration.

The radio was also changed, with the substitution of the TR9b radio for the Type 9c. This led to a change in aerial, the new one being enclosed in a streamlined casing, where the TR9b had simply had a wire aerial from the fin to a simple 'stick'-like aerial post.

The prototype had its exhaust ports open, as holes along the side of the cowling, and on production aeroplanes these were encased in three kidney-shaped stubs, each covering two ports, which gave some residual thrust from the hot exhaust gases. Later Mark Is were fitted with ejector exhausts, which did produce more flame at night, but added a further couple of knots to the top speed by angling the hot exhaust gases backwards.

The fabric-covered wings also gave some cause for concern. Although fine on biplanes with speeds of around 250mph (402km/h), the Hurricane could be dived in excess of 350mph (563km/h). At this speed, the fabric could be seen to balloon between the wing ribs as the low-pressure area over the wing pulled at the fabric. Work on the design of an all-metal wing had been started in 1935, but this was not put into production until after approximately eighty Hurricanes had been built. Several fabric-wing Hurricanes were still in service during the Battle of Britain, although a good number had had their wings replaced during servicing or after repair. Changing the wings only required three hours' work per aircraft.

The metal-skinned wings allowed a diving speed that was 80mph (129km/h) higher than the fabric-covered ones. They were very different in construction. Instead of the 'dumb-bell' spars and diagonal bracing, they were far more conventional, with spars consisting of extruded light alloy booms and the webs made from light alloy sheet. Ribs were made from extruded section and two additional stringers were fitted spanwise along the wing. The metal-skinned wings were interchangeable with the fabric-covered wings, and one trials Hurricane, L1877, was even flown with a fabric-covered port wing and metal-covered starboard wing. The great advantage of the metal-covered wings over the fabric ones was that the metal ones could carry far greater stress loads without needing so much structure beneath.

With war clouds looming, it was realized that the 37mm cannon on a Messerschmitt Bf 109E could do

Another early 'L' series Hurricane shows the port-side Venturi fitted beneath the windscreen. (*Aeroplane Monthly*)

considerable damage. In response, an armoured windscreen and armour protection for the pilot in front of and behind the cockpit were incorporated. A series of modifications was put into place, but many Hurricanes in the early months of the war, including some that went to France, were unarmoured. By the time of the Battle of Britain all had been converted.

Wartime

The outbreak of war was followed by the 'Phoney War' period, which gave the RAF a chance to build up its front-line strength with aircraft more modern than Gladiators or Gauntlets. The first major fighting was to take place in France, with the British Expeditionary Force setting out in early 1940. Initial engagements with the Luftwaffe showed the Hurricane to be a tight-turning and steady gun platform, but the Watts two-bladed propeller was clearly unsuitable. At least one pilot complained of how a Heinkel 111 was able to pull away from him in a chase, yet by this time the Heinkel was obsolescent!

Tests with three-bladed variable pitch propellers had taken place in August 1938. De Havilland was manufacturing the American Hamilton propeller under licence. This was a two-position propeller that gave a fine pitch setting for take-off and a coarse for cruise. Although nearly 300lb (136kg) heavier than the Watts, it greatly improved the Hurricane's rate of climb. The Rotol company, formed by Rolls-Royce and Bristol, was also making variable pitch propellers, although these were constant speed rather than two pitch. They were first tried on a Hurricane in

January 1939. This gave the Hurricane a better rate of climb and increased the top speed to 328mph (528km/h) at 16,200ft (4,940m). Rolls-Royce modified the Merlin to accept either the de Havilland or Rotol propeller, and this became known as the Merlin III.

A number of Hurricanes were retrofitted with de Havilland propellers, but the Rotol was chosen for production as this not only had the benefit of being more controllable, but was also lighter. The normal loaded weight of the aircraft with Rotol prop was 6,447lb (2,924kg) against 6,499lb (2,948kg) with the De Havilland.

Combat experience also showed that the pilot could be trapped in his cockpit if gunfire damaged the canopy rails. The answer was to fit a jettisonable hood. Rear-view mirrors were also added to the top of the windscreen to give some rearward visibility. Self-sealing covers were added to the fuselage fuel tank.

By the start of the Battle of Britain the Hurricane had been blooded in France and most of its teething problems had been cured. Hurricanes were also being produced in reasonable numbers, as Hawker was producing them at Kingston-upon-Thames and Brooklands, while Gloster was building them at Brockworth. T.O.M. Sopwith's decision to prepare for orders of 1,000 aircraft proved to have been inspired – by June 1940, 100 Hurricanes were being produced each week.

In combat, the Hurricane had been shown to be slightly slower than both the Spitfire I and II and the Messerschmitt Bf 190E, but it could out-turn both of

H.M. King George VI inspecting an early Hurricane during May 1938. The difference in tone between the metal-covered centre section and the fabric-covered outer wing is clear. Also of note is the Warren truss in the gun bay that is clearly twelve-sided, like the spars. This changed on later all-metal wings. Also clearly shown next to the undercarriage selector by the seat, is the handpump for the undercarriage system that had to be pumped up and down by the pilot. The gun bay opening also differs from the metal-wing Hurricane. Compare this photograph with those on page 66. (*Aeroplane Monthly*)

P3065 was hit during the Battle of Britain and force-landed with a wounded pilot. The damage to the undercarriage doors and missing radiator point to a belly landing. This Hurricane was written off. (*Aeroplane Monthly*)

A pilot races out to his bomb-equipped Hurricane IIA, possibly in Malta. The fishtail exhausts and longer spinner are of note. (*Aeroplane Monthly*)

them. It was also a steady gun platform and had already demonstrated its ruggedness as several had been badly damaged yet returned to base. It was possible to put bullets through a Hurricane and hit nothing of importance and to repair the damage with nothing more than a doped-on patch. However, damage to the metal-covered wings and tail or the primary structure was often a little more complicated.

The Hurricane was also well-suited to operation from rough fields and grass runways, where the wide-track undercarriage and relatively good view over the nose were appreciated by pilots.

One lesson learned in combat had been that even eight .303 machine guns would not guarantee a successful kill in the fast-moving air combats that were taking place. The first aircraft downed on the British Isles was a Heinkel 111 on 28 October 1939, shot down by the Spitfires of 602 squadron. The Heinkel had taken many hits and several of its crew were killed, yet it still managed a controlled crash-landing.

At Martlesham Heath in February 1939, Hawker had tested a Mark I, L1750, which had been modified with two 20mm Hispano cannon. The cannons were much heavier than the machine guns, which affected performance, and also were still some way from

being reliable enough for combat use. At least one cannon-armed Hurricane was tested operationally in 1940, but the cannon installation cut the top speed down to 291mph (468km/h) at 13,100ft (3,990m), hardly ideal in the existing combat situation.

The Hurricane II

The rapid development of the Merlin was to make a cannon-armed Hurricane a better proposition. Rolls-Royce was gradually increasing the power of the engine, and by mid-1940 had produced the Merlin XX. This engine was fitted with a two-speed supercharger blower that raised the ceiling of the engine and gave it 1,185hp, 155hp more than the Merlin III. The decision was made to introduce the new engine on to the production line as soon as Mark I contracts had been completed. The new variant was to be known as the Mark II. The new engine also had an additional advantage. Whereas the Merlin II and III engines used pure glycol for cooling, the Merlin XX used a mix of 30 per cent glycol and 70 per cent water. Pure glycol is flammable, so not only was the new mix safer, but the engine also ran approximately 70°C cooler, which gave longer engine life and greater reliability.

The new engine was longer than the earlier Merlin and so the Hurricane gained a 4.5in insert in front of the cockpit, which made the aircraft slightly more stable due to the slight forward shift in the centre of gravity.

Hawker was already working on the design of the Hawker Tornado and Typhoon, which were planned to have a twelve-gun wing. Hawker suggested to the Air Ministry that the Hurricane should be brought up to this standard by adding two guns outboard of the landing light. The Air Ministry was, at first, reluctant. The .303 Browning was required in large numbers, being the standard gun in most gun turrets and fighters, and so there was concern that placing extra guns on the Hurricane could lead to shortages. Therefore, the first 120 Hurricane IIs were flown with the original eight-gun wing, with the twelve-gun wing being introduced on to the lines at Langley in November 1940.

Some Mark IIs were also fitted with attachment points for 45-gallon (205ltr) long-range drop tanks. The Hurricane had been designed as an interceptor fighter whose role would be to scramble and get to height quickly in order to dispose of an enemy bombing force. The change in tactics that led first to standing patrols of aircraft and then to fighter sweeps across France highlighted a lack of range that was inherent in many interceptor designs, including the Spitfire.

The extra power available from the Merlin XX also allowed further development of the cannon-armed Hurricane. Although the experiments on Mark Is had shown the top speed to be less than 300mph (483km/h) the Mark IIC, with the new cannon wing, had a top speed of 336mph (541km/h). Mark IIA, B and C models were produced together on the lines. Aircraft with the eight-gun wing were designated with the suffix A, those with the twelve-gun wing were designated B and those with the four-cannon wing, C. The last Hurricane built, PZ865, was a Mark II fitted with the four-cannon wing, and therefore was designated a Mark IIC.

Rockets and Bigger Guns

By the end of 1941, the Hurricane was being outclassed by the new Messerschmitt Bf 109F and was really at the end of its development as a true interceptor fighter. The thick wing that was aerodynamically sound at speeds up to 350mph (563km/h) was beginning to run into problems of compressibility as diving speeds exceeded 400mph (644km/h). This was no fault of the Hawker design team, who had built the aeroplane to a specification that it exceeded with ease, but more an illustration of how fast developments were taking place at this time. The Spitfire had been designed with a thin wing from the outset, and although this gave it a higher speed potential, it had also caused problems in fitting the undercarriage and guns into the wing. Nor was the Spitfire as rugged as the Hurricane.

The steel tube fuselage of the Hurricane was also time-consuming to make. Using this method for the relatively small amounts of earlier biplanes had been fine, but in wartime mass production, often with semi-skilled labour, the effort needed to fit the countless pieces that connected each tube was not economic. The Tornado, the experimental forerunner of the Typhoon, and the Typhoon itself, had a tube front section to the

A bomb-equipped Hurricane II (or XII) B. The two extra gun ports can be seen outboard of the landing light. (*Aeroplane Monthly*)

This posed photograph from May 1945 gives a good view of the nose of a late Hurricane with tropical filter and the two-cannon 'C' armament. The recoil springs are clearly visible. (*Aeroplane Monthly*)

fuselage, which allowed excellent access to the cockpit area and engine controls, but it had a monocoque tail section. Even the thin-wing Typhoon, that later became the well-respected Tempest, was to have a forward fuselage built in the same way as the Hurricane. It was only in the very late stages of the war that Hawker produced its first and only monocoque fuselage single-piston engine fighter. This was subsequently refused by the RAF, but used to great effect by the Navy and a whole generation of unlimited air racers. It was the excellent Sea Fury.

The 20mm cannon in the Mark IIC was an effective air weapon, but also very good against ground targets. As the Hurricane was withdrawn from pure fighter operations, it found a highly effective new role in ground attack. After the Battle of Britain, the 'powers that be' were very keen take the war to the occupying forces in France. This was intended partly as a morale booster for a battered and tired British public who had endured the Blitz, but also to raise morale within Fighter Command and to lift them from the defensive stance they had been forced to assume during the Battle of Britain. The Hurricane was very effective against all but the most heavily

armoured vehicles and, to increase its firepower, trials with rocket projectiles were carried out in May 1942. The rockets were not particularly accurate but they were powerful. A salvo of eight rockets, as fitted to the Hurricane, is said to have had the same destructive power as a broadside from a Naval cruiser.

However, even the rocket projectile could not open up the most heavily armoured vehicles, and since 1939 both Rolls-Royce and Vickers had been working to produce a 40mm gun that could be mounted in a fighter aircraft. By 1941 these designs were well advanced, and the Hurricane II was showing itself capable of carrying four 20mm cannon. A trial installation was made in a Hurricane IIA with ten of the Brownings being deleted, the other two remaining to carry tracer ammunition to aid in sighting the cannon. Trials showed some problems with the Rolls-Royce gun, which was then discontinued, and all efforts concentrated on the Vickers 'S' gun.

Further armour was also fitted to the 40mm cannon Hurricane, which became known as the Mark IID, and the outer-wing attachments were strengthened so that 4G could be pulled at a weight of 8,540lb (3,874kg).

Although outclassed in the European theatre, the Hurricane was to carry on as a front-line fighter in other Commands. By 1941 the Hurricane had already fought in France and Norway, though it had to withdraw in both cases. Churchill's policy of keeping Spitfires at home led to Hurricanes being embarked on HMS *Argus* for the trip to Malta to bolster the Island's defences that had been relying on the remains of the locally based Sea Gladiators, which had become known as Faith, Hope and Charity. The Hurricanes were hard pressed by the attacking Luftwaffe and Reggia Aeronautica fighters, but performed well, being ideally suited to the rough conditions.

As the Hurricane slipped from front-line fighter use it found a new role as a ground-attack aircraft. The four 20mm cannon on the Mark IIC were a formidable weapon against soft-skinned vehicles and railway wagons and in 1941 the Hurricane IIB and IIC were fitted with racks allowing them to carry two 250lb or two 500lb bombs. This lowered the top speed of the Hurricane to 301mph (484km/h), but by this point mixed sweeps of Hurricanes protected by a fighter screen of Spitfires were not uncommon. The same racks would allow the Hurricane to carry either two 45-gallon (205ltr) or two 90-gallon (410ltr) drop tanks, more than doubling the Hurricane's fuel load.

Photo Reconnaissance

Although Spitfires were proving to be very useful photo-reconnaissance (PR) aircraft, they were not available in some theatres of war. In Egypt, the Service Depot at Heliopolis converted some Hurricane Is for the role. The first three were converted in January 1941. Two carried a pair of F24 cameras with 8in focal length lenses and the third a vertical and two oblique F24s with 14in focal length lenses in the rear fuselage. The cameras were mounted in the rear fuselage close to the trailing edge of the wing and a fairing was built up over the lenses aft of the radiator housing. A further five Hurricanes were modified in March 1941, while two were converted in a similar manner in Malta during April 1941.

During October 1941, a batch of six Hurricane IIs was converted to PR Mark II status, and a final batch, thought to be of twelve aircraft, was converted in late 1942. Many of these were shipped to India to be part of No.3 PRU (photo reconnaissance unit). The limited number of airframes, roughly thirty-six, and the localized conversion mean that few photographs exist. The PR Mark II was said to be capable of slightly over 350mph (563km/h) and was able to reach 38,000ft (11,580m).

For duties closer to the front lines, some Hurricanes were converted to Tactical Reconnaissance (Tac R) aircraft. While the Hurricane had not been designed as a close-support fighter, it proved itself to be very capable. Often these aircraft would be called in to deal with localized opposition, and so an additional radio transmitter was fitted for liaison with ground forces who were better placed to direct the Hurricane to deal with the enemy. Some Tac R conversions also had a vertical camera fitted in the rear fuselage, so to compensate for the extra weight either one or two Brownings would be omitted on the Mark I versions and two cannons on the Mark II. It was not possible to remove just one cannon as asymmetric firing was more of a problem than with machine guns. Externally, these aircraft are only distinguishable by the missing armament.

The Hurricane Goes to Sea

The first Hurricanes to operate from ships were those of No. 46 Squadron, which were flown from HMS *Glorious* in July 1940 to fight in Norway. After the withdrawal of British forces, the survivors of these aircraft were flown back to HMS *Glorious*, where they landed despite the pilots having no experience in deck landings and there being no arrester gear. Sadly, this was to no avail as although the Hurricanes were saved from destruction when the German forces overran Norway, they were lost when *Glorious* was sunk soon after.

Hurricanes had been flown from the carrier HMS *Argus* to reinforce Malta during August 1940 and the feasibility of operating the Hurricane as a Naval fighter did not go unnoticed.

The first Hurricanes that went to sea were not designed to land back on to anything. Air attacks on convoys were causing massive problems and one answer was to fit a catapult to the front of a merchant ship with a Hurricane ready for launch. When an intruder was spotted the Hurricane could be launched to defend the convoy. If this was successful and the convoy was close to land, the Hurricane could make its way back to a shore base, but at sea the Hurricane pilot would be forced to bail out or to ditch. Both of these options had their problems – there was always a chance of striking part of the fuselage when bailing out and a number of pilots had been killed in this way. On the other hand, ditching the Hurricane was problematic too. The radiator housing acted as a water brake, pitching the nose of the fighter downwards when it hit the water, while also acting as a very efficient scoop, helping to flood the inside of the Hurricane so that a quick exit was advisable before the aeroplane sank. The pilot then had to survive in freezing water while a boat was sent for him.

The ships used were either known as Fighter

A western desert Hurricane sporting tropical filter, but with the early Fighter Command black and white undersides. It is dated 7 November 1940 and the pilot is identified on the photograph as P/O Lapsley. (*Aeroplane Monthly*)

Catapult Ships, which were Naval Auxiliary Vessels crewed by Naval personnel whose aircraft were operated by the Fleet Air Arm, or as Catapult Armed Merchantmen, or CAM ships, whose crews were entirely civilian and whose Hurricanes were crewed and serviced by RAF personnel. In both cases, the Hurricanes were taken from stocks of former front-line Mark Is that were hardly in the best condition since they were considered expendable. These conversions, which numbered approximately 250 aircraft, were known as Sea Hurricane Mark IA.

Converting the Hurricane into a true carrier fighter took a little more effort than had been expended on the Sea Hurricane Mark IA. The catapult spools used on the CAM ship Hurricanes were retained and the fuselage restressed and strengthened to take an A-frame arrester hook, which was attached to the bottom longerons roughly a third of the way between the wing trailing edge and the tailwheel, and which was recessed into a cutout in the ventral fin beneath the fuselage.

In all, more than eighty modifications were needed to convert a Hurricane into a Sea Hurricane, includ-

ing new radios to conform with those used by the Fleet Air Arm and new instrumentation to read in knots rather than miles per hour.

Tropical Noses

The need to protect British interests in the Middle East, in particular free passage through the Mediterranean and Suez Canal for ships passing to and from India, Singapore and other parts of the Empire, meant that the RAF kept a reasonable force in the area. By the beginning of World War II, much of the equipment was obsolete. This had been fine for operations against tribal cultures, but to protect the area from German and Italian forces, more modern equipment would be needed. By 1938, there was a pressing need to prepare Hurricanes for operation in the desert should this be required.

The aggressive nature of desert sand caused considerable engine wear when the aircraft were taking off and landing and operating at low level. To prevent ingestion of the dust, tropical filters from the Vokes company and from Rolls-Royce were tested with one Hurricane, with a Vokes filter being transported to Khartoum for desert trials.

The collapse of France and entry of Italy into the war in June 1940 made deployment of Hurricanes to the area a priority. During August, Hurricanes were sent to Malta and to Egypt. Early deliveries consisted of somewhat tired former front-line Hurricanes that had been flown in France and in the early stages of the Battle of Britain. They were delivered without the tropical filters, and so the engines suffered further until these were fitted. Other tropical equipment fitted included a water bottle behind the cockpit to help the pilot survive in the event of a forced landing in the desert.

The Hurricane IV

The variety of armament carried by the Hurricane meant that there were many variations in the wing. A 'universal' wing, which could be easily configured in a variety of ways, was therefore desirable. Work was started on the Hurricane IIE, but was stopped when it was realized that the Hurricane was better deployed in the Middle and Far East than in Europe. Rolls-Royce produced the Merlin 27, which had a redesigned oil system that was better suited to operation in the tropics, and which was rated at a slightly lower altitude in keeping with the Hurricane's new role as a close-support fighter.

The prototype Mark IV was a converted Mark II that was initially fitted with a Merlin 32 and a four-bladed prop. The radiator was deeper and armoured. The armament on the prototype was a pair of 40mm

Vickers guns, but the wings could accommodate 3in rocket projectiles, 40mm anti-tank guns, drop tanks and 250lb and 500lb bombs. Additional armour was also fitted around the engine.

The final variant to be produced was the Mark V, although only three were built and it never reached production. This was powered by a Merlin 32 boosted to give 1,700hp at low level and was intended as a dedicated ground-attack aeroplane for use in Burma. All three prototypes were fitted with four-bladed propellers and one was measured at 326mph (525km/h) at 500ft, which is comparable with the Hurricane I despite being over one and a half times as heavy.

Production

Production of the Hurricane was a major achievement given the conditions under which it was undertaken.

The roots of the Hurricane production story lie with the famous World War I company, the Sopwith Aviation Company. The Sopwith company had started building aircraft in the old roller-skating rink at Kingston-upon-Thames, Surrey, in 1909. The expansion during World War I caused Sopwith to look for additional premises, and these were found in the Canbury Park Road area of Kingston. Sopwith bought up the freehold on the land in 1914, with local estate agents persuading many of the tenants of the small cottages on the site to leave.

The old Sopwith company had grown beyond all expectations during World War I, but when War Office contracts were cancelled at the end of the war, the company had no choice but to go into liquidation. The H.G. Hawker Engineering Company was created immediately as a general engineering company. It was named after 'Harry' Hawker, Sopwith's chief pilot and T.O.M. Sopwith's right-hand man. The company also supported the Sopwith Snipe, which was still in service with the RAF and the Camel, which was still in service with the Royal Navy.

The company also undertook subcontract work for other aircraft manufacturers and refurbished aircraft for the RAF and for export. However, it was always T.O.M. Sopwith's intention that the company should attain the position that had been enjoyed by the Sopwith Aviation Company as a prime supplier of aircraft for the Services.

As the new company grew, a design office was started and its first significant aircraft was the Hawker Woodcock, of which sixty-seven were built between 1923 and 1927. By 1926, the Hawker Horsley was in production as a bomber and torpedo aircraft, and 123 of these were built. These aircraft were designed by W.G. Carter, who would later

design the Gloster Meteor. He was assisted by Sydney Camm, who had joined Hawker's in 1923.

The most significant aircraft of the period was the Hawker Heron, of which only one prototype was built, but it was the first Hawker aircraft with a primary structure of metal. This construction was also used on the Hawker Tomtit trainer and by 1927 it had been developed to the stage where it could be used on a heavier aircraft, the Hawker Hart.

By 1924, The H.G. Hawker Engineering Company had reoccupied most of the old Sopwith buildings. The 150,000sq ft Canbury Park Road factory was hardly ideal for aircraft production as it was on three main floors and internally these floor levels varied across the site, so that ramps and steps were needed to get around even on one floor. The staircases between floors were steep and hazardous if carrying parts, which was sometimes necessary as the goods lift was very slow.

The main floor area of 20,000sq ft served as an erection shop where fuselages were built and equipped. These were fabric-covered and doped in a separate workshop at the eastern end of the building. Sheet metal work and the rolling of components was also carried out in this area, which, unlike many of the workshops on the site, benefited from natural light. Also on the ground floor were the stores, millwrights' department and machine shop, with the woodworking shop and sawmill at the northern end of the site. At one end of the machine shop there was a Hawker-designed plant for making the streamline flying wires that had to be rolled from stainless steel bar.

The first floor consisted of the plane shop, where wing panels were built up on trestles, with the parts being made up in peripheral areas. On the top floor was the fitters' shop.

The old skating rink was reoccupied and used to build development aircraft, with the prototype Hurricane being built there in 1935. A new building was constructed on the south side of Canbury Park Road in 1933 to house the experimental department, with a tool room on the first floor and a canteen above. As the company expanded, the tool room was moved to the skating rink and both the first and second floors of the new building were used as canteens. Next to this building was a warehouse, originally built for the local department store Bentalls as a furniture depository, and this was acquired in the mid-1930s to house the stores, with the top floor becoming the design office.

Aircraft were built here and transported in pieces to Brooklands aerodrome at Weybridge in Surrey for final assembly and testing. Here, Hawker's had a

Many of the Hawker biplanes were assembled in Vicker's factory at Weybridge. This view shows Hart and Hart Trainer fuselages in 1933. The similarities to the Hurricane frame are evident. (*Aeroplane Monthly*)

30,000sq ft former RAF 'Belfast' hanger of World War I vintage (the same design as those surviving at the Imperial War Museum at Duxford in Cambridgeshire).

As production increased in the years leading up to World War II, the haphazard layout of the Kingston factory was clearly unsuitable as not only was it inefficient, but the factory was also in the middle of a densely populated area. A new erection shop was built at Brooklands on the site of the pre-World War I sheds close to the Byfleet banking. This new building allowed for five rows of Hurricane fuselages to be assembled and covered.

When the Hawker board took the bold decision to tool up for 1,000 aircraft before an order had been received, it was realized that further production facilities would be required. This was not only because of the amount of Hurricanes involved, but also because much of the machinery and plant at Kingston was old and worn, and the Hurricane required a greater degree of accuracy in its construction than had been the case with some of the previous aircraft constructed by the company.

In 1936 company test pilots had been asked to look out for suitable sites, and a site at Langley, close to

Slough, was chosen. A 600,000sq ft factory was started there in 1937 and this was occupied from June 1939. As production increased and repair work was added, it was extended to 750,000sq ft. The first Hurricane was delivered from Langley in October 1939, while Kingston and Brooklands continued to produce a large number.

The political situation during 1936–7 made it evident that further production was needed, and so in September 1937 Gloster Aircraft Limited, a company that had been bought by Hawker's in 1933, was given a contract for 500 Hurricanes. The first of these flew in October 1939. Gloster also produced metal wings to replace the fabric wings on many Brooklands-built Hurricanes.

The Austin Motor Company also built one batch of 300 Mark IIB and IIC Hurricanes in 1940–41 at its plant at Longbridge on the outskirts of Oxford.

Canadian Hurricanes

During 1938, the Canadian government agreed to undertake Hurricane production at the Canadian Car and Foundry Company in Montreal. Hawker supplied

Britain's oldest ally, Portugal, took delivery of forty Hurricane IICs after World War II. These were taken from RAF stocks and overhauled at Langley before shipment. They are fitted with long-range tanks for the ferry flight. (*Aeroplane Monthly*)

drawings, one set of components and one complete aircraft as a pattern and the Canadian company did the rest. The tooling was completed in early 1939 and the first aircraft was flown in January 1940. Canadian Car and Foundry went on to produce 1,451 Hurricanes in several marks.

Early Canadian Hurricanes were built as Mark Is with Merlin IIIs and eight-gun wings, but later marks were fitted with the Packard-built Merlin 28 or 29. Eight- and twelve-gun wings and four-cannon wings were also made. Many of the aircraft were built with American Hamilton Standard Hydromatic propellers and a number were either built as, or converted to, Sea Hurricanes. There is evidence that Sea Hurricanes flew with the Royal Canadian Air Force and non-navalized Hurricanes with the Royal Canadian Navy. Some Canadian-built Hurricanes were also operated by the United States Army Air Force.

Foreign production was also started in Belgium, where two aircraft were completed before the country was overrun by the invading German forces. In Belgrade, twenty aircraft were completed before the occupation.

Subcontracting Production

At home, subcontract work was an important part of the wartime aircraft industry, and Hawker planned to use 50 per cent of details and sub-assemblies from outside suppliers. These included the wings from Gloster that have already been mentioned, as well as from a host of smaller companies. Wings were also built by the LMS railway company and Scottish

Motor Traction at Airdrie, but production problems led to this work being transferred back to Langley.

As production increased, the factories instigated night shifts and were forced to find even more space. Bomb damage to the Progress department on the north side of the Canbury Park Road plant (only one bomb actually hit the Kingston works) caused the experimental drawing office and some other departments to move to Claremont House in nearby Esher for the duration of the war. Hawker's also took over other buildings in the Kingston area for storage and small assembly work.

As the Langley factory increased production, the old factory at Brooklands was run down and eventually passed to Vickers in 1941. Production at Langley was eventually on five lines, with the aircraft on wheeled trolleys so that they could be moved along the line. As one was taken off the end of each line another would be started. Peak production at Langley amounted to eight aircraft per day in the second quarter of 1942. The actual time on the line varied slightly, but was estimated to be forty-five days.

Construction Sequence

The fuselage was made of five sub-assembled units. First to be constructed was the centre section of the fuselage, which was constant width and provided the basis for aligning the rest of the fuselage.

The rear fuselage was built up as two side frames that tapered in plan, and at the rear of this was a smaller, and more sharply tapered, section that carried the fin, tailplane and tailwheel attachments.

Two two-seater Hurricanes were built for the Persian Air Force in 1947. The rear cockpit was fitted with a sliding hood from a Tempest, while the student in the front had to go without! (*Aeroplane Monthly*)

The fuselage was then mounted on a jig that represented the wing centre section spars, and the cross tubes and bracing wires, which for some reason on the internal structure were streamlined, were installed and adjusted to give correct alignment at the tail. This was checked with a plumb bob to a datum plate on the floor of the factory. The fuselage was then removed from the jig ready for mounting on to its proper centre section. At this stage, much of the internal equipment could be fitted, such as controls and cabling, prior to fitting the wooden formers and stringers that made up the outer shape of the fuselage.

The fabric-covered outer wings for the Hurricane were mostly built at Kingston on upright jigs that conveniently fitted into the upright girders in the old furniture depository building. The all-metal wings on the Mark I were mostly built by Gloster and later at Langley. These too were built in jigs that were held vertically with the nose down and were built in pairs. Completion of the leading edge and other parts that were more accessible with the wing horizontal were done with the wings on trestles.

The centre section was built up in a jig to ensure proper alignment and the fuselage was mounted on to this. The radiator, fuel and oil tanks and associated piping were installed; the undercarriage and the engine, engine mount and firewall were also installed at this time. The woodwork would also be added.

The fuselage could then be moved on its own wheels to the covering and paint shop. From there, it would go for final finishing, with the tailplane and rudder, windscreen and the covering panels being added. The fuselage would then go to the flight shed, where outer wings, armament and radios would be added. It was also prepared for flight-testing. Following flight-testing, the Hurricane would be ferried to an RAF Maintenance Unit, where any recent field modifications would be incorporated and the final items of military equipment added. The Hurricane was now ready to be issued to a squadron.

In all, 14,533 Hurricanes were produced, and today survivors can be seen in the United Kingdom, United States of America, Canada and India. Several wrecks from Russia have been recovered and some are being restored to airworthy condition by companies such as Hawker Restorations in Suffolk, who have produced several airworthy Hurricanes and have supplied parts and expertise for several more. With their level of expertise it is likely that the Hurricane will be seen in the skies for many more years.

Fuselage

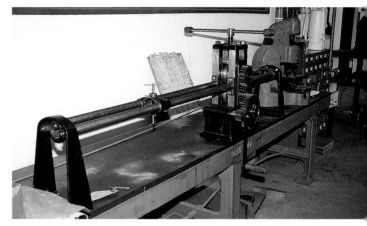

The tube-squaring machine at Hawker Restorations in Milden, Suffolk, is an exact copy of the original from Hawker's Kingston factory.

The first stage in the fuselage building process is to flatten the ends of the tubes to take the stainless steel joining plates.

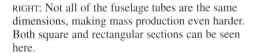

RIGHT: Not all of the fuselage tubes are the same dimensions, making mass production even harder. Both square and rectangular sections can be seen here.

The complexity of even one of the more simple fuselage joins can be seen. The longerons are fully square with the uprights being rectangular. The fishplate is bolted to the longeron, with the bolt going through a spacer pushed into the end of the tube to prevent it from being crushed. The uprights are held with hollow rivets. On the inside is a bracket to attach the bracing wires.

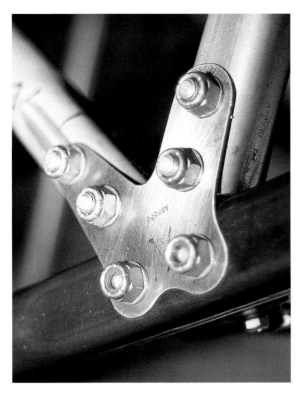

Not all the tubes get hollow rivets. This joint is all bolted and is shown whilst trial-fitted prior to the frame being painted. When this is assembled properly the lower bolts will be of the correct length – those fitted here would not pass inspection!

The internal spacer that prevents the tube from crushing can be seen here. This has to be an interference fit, with no play whatsoever. Hole centres on the tubes need to be accurate to within three thousandths of an inch.

The inside of a fuselage cross piece. The streamlined bracing wires fit into the brackets that are bolted to the fishplates.

A rear fuselage being test-assembled at Hawker Restorations Ltd.

The rear fuselage has a trestle point built into one of the joining fishplates.

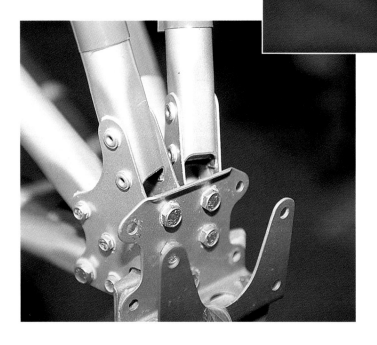

The rear of the fuselage tapers to meet the dumb-bell sternpost, which is held by this U-bracket.

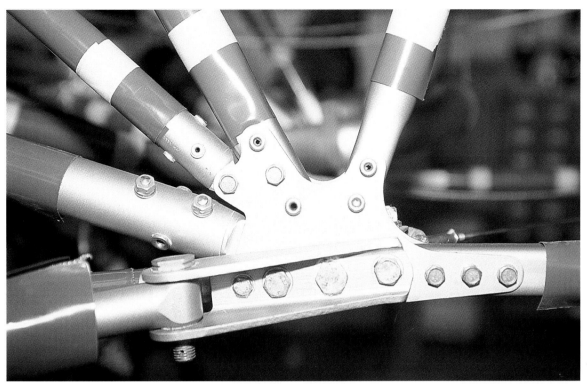

ABOVE: The complexity of some of the fuselage joins is clear from this photograph of the frame at the rear of the centre section.

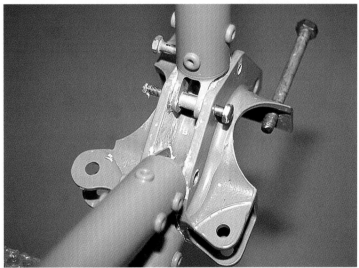

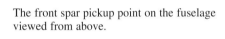

The front spar pickup point on the fuselage viewed from above.

The centre section is attached at an early stage to allow systems and controls to be installed. The complex spar fitting is seen here at the top and is bolted through the upper boom of the spar.

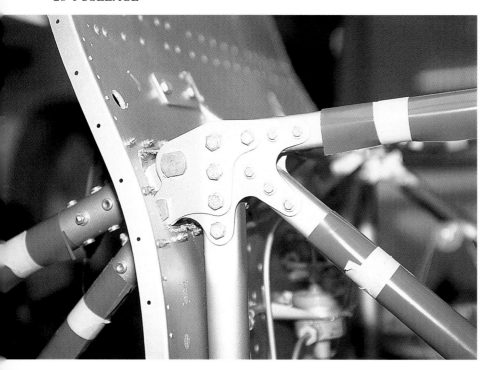

This picture of the engine mount to firewall join is another example of how complicated the joints in a Hurricane could be. In this photograph, the engine mount is off to the left and the fuselage to the right.

ABOVE: The tailplane attachment fitting is fixed to the very rear of the main frame. This view also shows the join with the very rear section.

The footstep on the Hurricane is retractable but also operates the handhold in the fuselage. As the footstep is pulled down a system of cables and bungees operate the handhold and also act as a return spring to help get the footstep back into place. The whole assembly can be a little fierce and it is not wise to get fingers in the way.

Centre Section

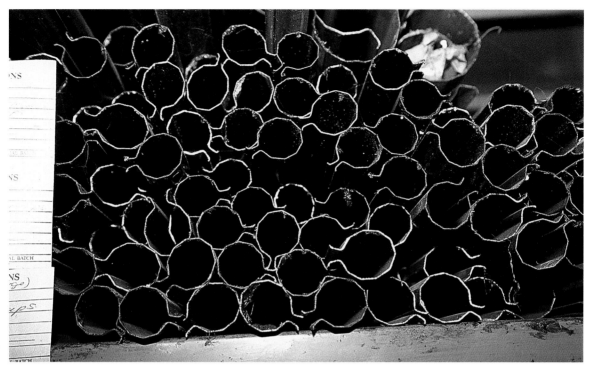

The spars on the Hurricane are made up of a twelve-sided rolled steel tube that is flanged to allow it to be fixed to the spar web. This is a store of spar material at Hawker Restorations. Several sizes are needed, as not only are the spars, fin and tailplane spars different, but the wing spars are made up from two pieces that fit one inside the other. At the root ends there is a further strengthening tube that runs through the centre and which takes the fittings that support the outer wing. Several sizes of rolled tube are seen here. The material proved difficult to obtain. The specification calls for T50 steel which is rated at 50 tons per inch tensile strength, but only T45 is now available. Hawker Engineering had to re-test batches of T45 to check if it conformed to the T50 Specification and then re-certify it as T50. This alone was hugely expensive.

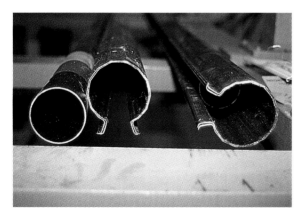 

The spar material laid out to demonstrate construction. Both the inner and outer twelve-sided spar booms can be seen around the inner steel tube. The engineering that is required to make this is superb as tolerances are very tight.

The first stage in the wing building process is to build the spars in the jig. The booms are riveted to the steel web. Once this has been done on both spars, the vertical supports and the inter-spar compression ribs and other fittings can be added before the centre section is removed from the jig and mated with the fuselage.

The newly rebuilt centre section is joined to the fuselage to ensure everything lines up.

The centre section front spar viewed from the front. The vertical stiffeners on the web can be seen and these are much larger where the outer wings attach, where the fuselage attaches and where the additional diagonal fuselage strut is located. The bolts through the spar that hold the central tube in place can also be seen.

BELOW: The number of parts in the Hurricane is easily visible with this view of the outer wing attachment point. The fittings that take the outer wing are inserted into the central spar tube and bolted into place. The larger vertical stiffener has lightening holes and on top of the spar, the framework that will take the outer skin is held in place temporarily with masking tape.

The inner surface of the spar is similar. In this view the compression ribs, made in the same way as the fuselage, can be seen, as can the first few parts of the undercarriage retraction mechanism.

The spar fitting on the left wing. The top-hat section to take the skin over the compression rib can be seen and to the left the oil tank is *in situ* as part of the wing leading edge.

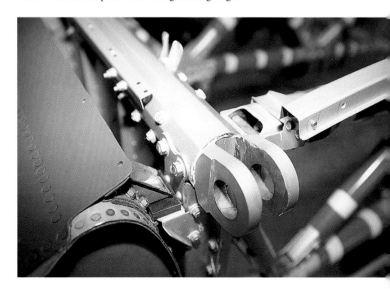

The compression ribs in the centre section are built up in the same way as the fuselage frame. They are also shaped to allow space for the undercarriage to retract. Many of the fittings and parts of this centre section will be used again.

An end-on view of the starboard wing showing the compression ribs, the skin attachment pieces, the leading edge and the undercarriage retraction. The inside of the wheel well wall can be seen towards the front of the wing and behind this will be the wing fuel tank.

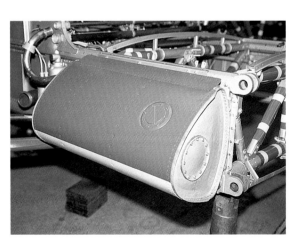

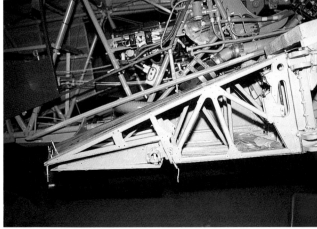

The oil tank makes up the leading edge of the port centre section.

The back half of the wing shows the flap in place on the under surface and the structure of the rear section.

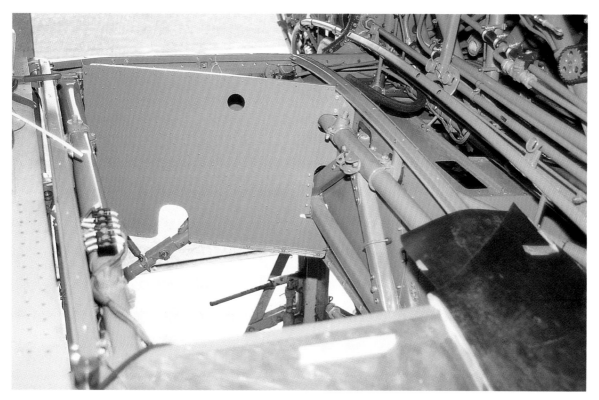

ABOVE: The wing fuel tank bay.

A wing fuel tank ready for installation. The hole though the tank takes one of the wing bracing wires.

The rear spar pick-up point with the wing in place. It is clear that damage to this component would have been far from easy to fix in the field.

Outer Wings

ABOVE: Airframe Assemblies, an Isle of Wight-based company that have produced several sets of wings for Hurricane rebuilds, used a lot of original parts to make patterns for new material. Here, the original section of spar web and the replacement are seen. The large circular openings are to take the machine gun blast tubes. A bullet hole is visible in the original panel close to the bottom on the right-hand side and a pencilled girl's name, presumably left by an assembly worker, is in the middle of the panel. (Chris Michell)

LEFT: A set of Hurricane spars for stressed-skin wings in the workshops of Airframe Assemblies. (Chris Michell)

ABOVE: The spar ends that bolt to the centre section were originally forgings, but for modern rebuilds are machined from solid. (Chris Michell)

LEFT: Various styles of wing ribs are used in the stressed skin wings. These are rib sections from about halfway along the wing. (Chris Michell)

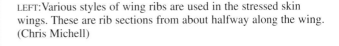

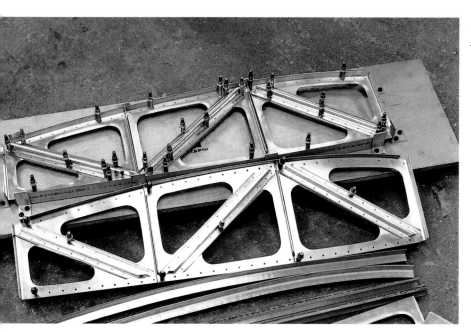

Outer wing rib sections in the jig. (Chris Michell)

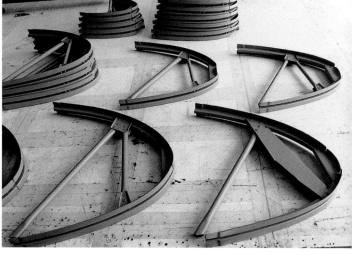

ABOVE: The nose ribs. On the outer wings these taper towards the tip. (Chris Michell)

A closer view of the wing spars. The ports for the machine guns can be seen and between them is the mounting for the diagonal ribs that is the only structural piece left from the fabric wing construction. (Chris Michell)

As wing assembly progresses, the centre ribs are added to the spars in the wing jig. (Chris Michell)

Different rib styles in the wing. The nearest have slots for the spanwise stringers. (Chris Michell)

Although the fabric wing of the Hurricane had diagonal Warren bracing along its length, this was only retained in the all-metal wings in the area of the machine-gun bays, and only then because changing this would have meant redesigning the machine-gun mounts. (Chris Michell)

With spanwise stringers in place, the first sections of wing skin are trial-fitted. (Chris Michell)

This view of the wing shows the nose ribs and trailing edge in place and the machine-gun mountings in the wing. (Chris Michell)

ABOVE: Skinning the wing continues out to the tips. Just visible here is the different construction of the ribs near the tip. (Chris Michell)

The wing skins are added and riveted into place. The Hurricane wing has mushroom-headed rivets over much of the structure. (Chris Michell)

With just the nose to be skinned, this wing is almost complete. (Chris Michell)

ABOVE: Skinning the machine-gun ports. (Chris Michell)

With most of the skin in place, the wing can be removed from the jig without distortion and the nose ribs are checked before skinning. (Chris Michell)

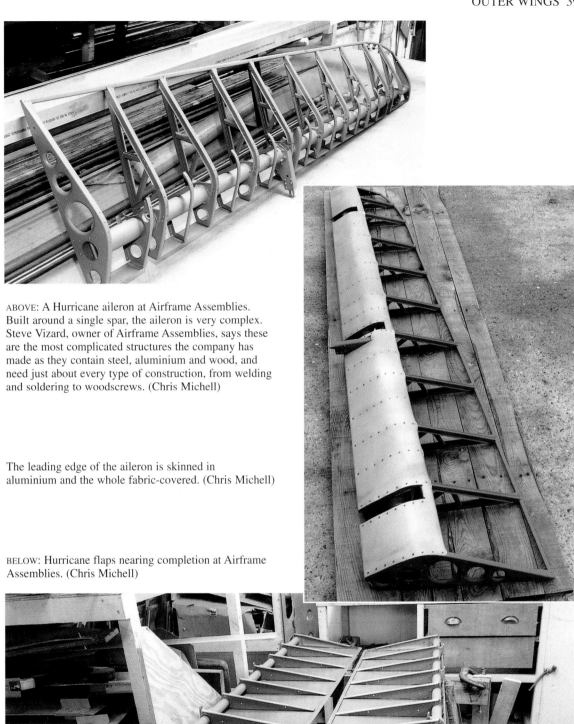

ABOVE: A Hurricane aileron at Airframe Assemblies. Built around a single spar, the aileron is very complex. Steve Vizard, owner of Airframe Assemblies, says these are the most complicated structures the company has made as they contain steel, aluminium and wood, and need just about every type of construction, from welding and soldering to woodscrews. (Chris Michell)

The leading edge of the aileron is skinned in aluminium and the whole fabric-covered. (Chris Michell)

BELOW: Hurricane flaps nearing completion at Airframe Assemblies. (Chris Michell)

LEFT: The Science Museum in London now houses the oldest surviving Hurricane. L1592 was part of the first production batch built at Brooklands in 1938. It served over Dunkirk and on 28 August 1940 was hit by a Bf 109 and forced to land at Croydon. It is still fitted with the early radio mast and fabric wings and is seen here on display at Horse Guards Parade in the 1950s.

RIGHT: The Science Museum Hurricane is almost impossible to photograph, and difficult even to see clearly, as the museum has a midnight-blue roof and is lit with spotlights. The rib positions can just be seen in this view of the upper wing.

The underside of L1592 is slightly easier to see and shows up the fabric, complete with repairs. This Hurricane was used in taxiing scenes in the 1952 film *Angels One Five* and was refurbished by Hawker's prior to being installed in the museum in 1963.

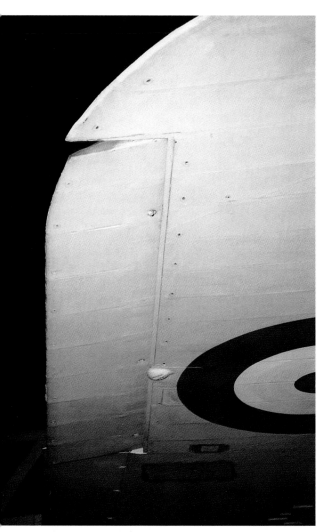

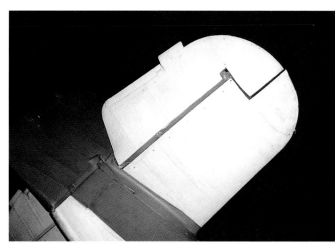

ABOVE: The underside of the tailplane shows the join between upper surface and lower surface colours on the elevator along the bottom edge of the leading edge, so that the lower surface colour does not show when the elevator is at full deflection when seen from above.

LEFT: Like all fabric-covered aiframes, the Hurricane has drain holes in the fabric along the trailing edge and before the aileron cut-out.

BELOW: The wing ribs on early fabric-wing Hurricanes were made with a channel into which the fabric was placed. Another channel section was then screwed into this to hold the fabric in place. This was then covered with fabric tape to give a smoother finish than would have been the case with conventional rib stitching. The discolouration of the landing light cover is also of note.

With the skin removed, the structure of this Mark IIB wing can be seen. (Chris Michell)

BELOW: This Hurricane wreck from Russia showed some interesting changes. The ejector ports for the eight machine guns are seen in this view of the wing undersurface. Just outboard of these can be seen four holes that were used to mount a bomb gear that was a field modification. Outboard of these, the additional ports for the outer guns on this twelve-gun wing can be seen. (Chris Michell)

LEFT AND ABOVE LEFT: This Hurricane IIC wing shows the cannons still in place. Noticeable is the absence of the diagonal members in the gun bay. (Chris Michell)

Tail

The construction of the tail is clear in this view of a tail recovered from a crash site. Although this looks to be nothing more than scrap it will provide many pieces that can be used in an airworthy rebuild. All parts are cleaned, inspected and tested before use.

ABOVE RIGHT: Part of the reason this Hurricane ceased to be a Hurricane and became a Hurricane wreck is due to this bullet hole through the tailplane spar.

This view of the crashed tail shows the front spar for the fin and the bottom rib that is fitted where the fin meets the fuselage.

BELOW: The tailplane spars are slightly simpler than the wing. This is the end of one spar with single rolled tubes riveted to the spring steel spar web.

LEFT: The restored tail on this Hurricane shows the construction and many of the features visible in the crashed example. Also visible is the trim mechanism, the fin to tail fairing and the metal leading edge of the tailplane.

RIGHT: The rear fuselage also has the jacking point built into the lower longeron. A rod can be passed through to sit on jacks.

BELOW: The rear of the fuselage frame has an additional section that tapers to the sternpost. The tailwheel oleo strut is the silver tube in the centre.

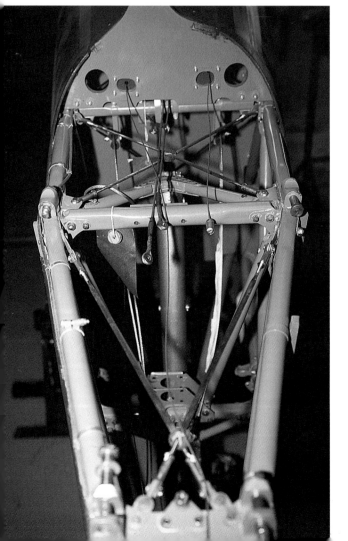

ABOVE: A side view of the tail with the fin in place. The rudder extension is visible, although the under-fuselage fairing is yet to be fitted.

This side view of the tail shows the access panel for the tail-wheel mechanism and rudder connections.

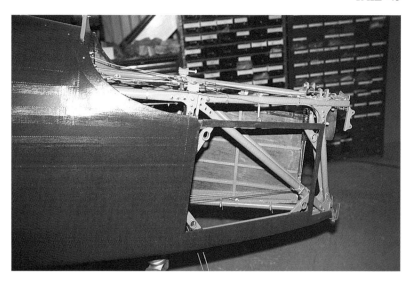

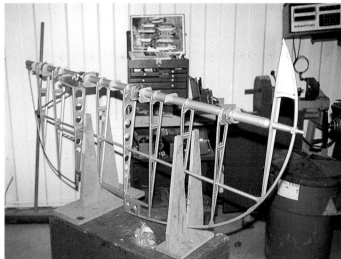

LEFT: A Hurricane fin showing the tubular spar and the ribs. The lead mass balance can also be seen with (above) a close-up of the mass balance weight on the fin.

BELOW: The tail trial-assembled for the fuselage to tail fairings to be fitted.

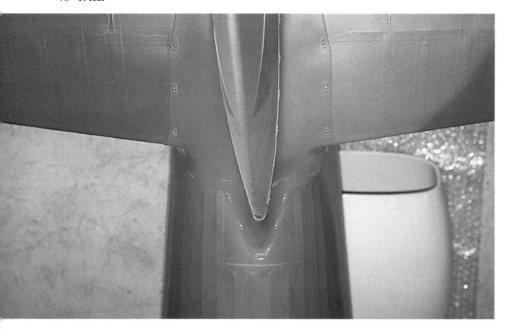

This vertical view of the tail shows the fin fairings and the slight offset of the fin to counteract engine torque.

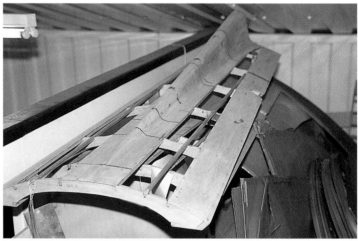

RIGHT: The anti-spin strake beneath the fuselage, which also acts as a tailwheel fairing, is built up on a wooden frame.

This overview of the elevator shows the relative positions of the trim tab and the gaps between the elevator and tailplane.

Fuselage Detail Assembly

The fuselage frame on the centre section with the radiator installed so that the pipework can be measured and built.

BELOW: Much of the internal plumbing is installed at an early stage. The radiator is installed here and the piping is being fitted. The main glycol pipe is supported temporarily whilst the fittings and connections are made.

ABOVE: A Hurricane coolant radiator ready for fitting. The circular hole for the oil cooler is clearly visible, as are the fixing brackets on the side and the pipe connections above.

The pipework at the front of the radiator shows the large diameter coolant pipes going into the glycol radiator, with the smaller oil pipes going into the central circular oil cooler.

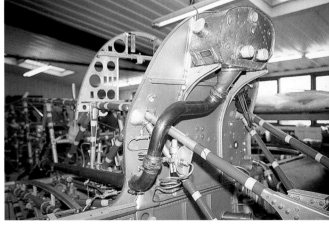

The engine mount can again be seen in this photograph, which also shows the glycol header tank for the cooling system in place on the firewall.

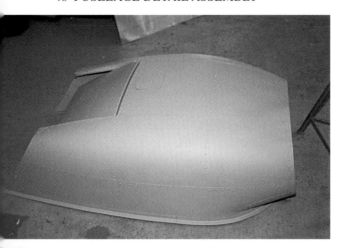

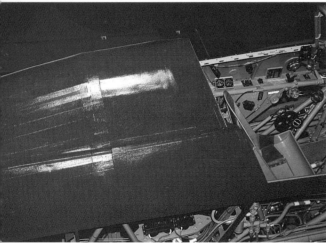

ABOVE: The doghouse is cut back to allow space for the hood to slide back. This view also shows the fabric covering extending from the plywood doghouse to the wooden rear fuselage stringers.

BELOW RIGHT: The panels towards the front of the fuselage are metal and are fitted to Dzus fasteners directly on to the frame. Those behind the cockpit are fitted into the wooden fairing and are made on wooden frames, then fabric-covered.

BELOW: This access panel is typical construction, with a wooden frame with fabric cover.

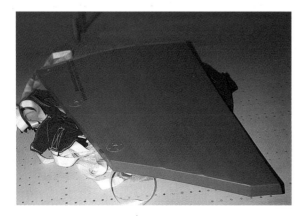

The radiator is enclosed in a metal fairing with a movable flap at the rear that can control the flow of air through the core. This is a brand new radiator housing waiting to be fitted.

BELOW: The cockpit area is surrounded by what is known as the doghouse. This is a ply structure that is built up over wooden frames and then covered with a thin fabric known as medapolam. The cockpit area on this Hurricane is red doped ready to accept the main fuselage fabric over the top.

ABOVE: The main fuselage contours are made up by wooden frames fixed to the main frame with wooden stringers. In this view the depth of the radio mast can also be seen.

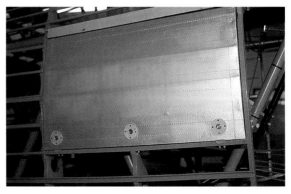

With the fuselage frame attached to the centre section, and the doghouse, frames and stringers in place, the familiar shape of the Hurricane begins to appear. In this view, the radio access panel behind the cockpit is fitted and silver-doped and the first of the wing root fairings is being fitted. The large pipe running along the side of the cockpit goes from the radiator to the coolant header tank.

The basic construction of the Hurricane is clear in this view of the right side of the fuselage. The basic frame runs along the bottom of the emergency access panel on the doghouse and the large cluster join that attaches the engine mount is to the right of centre. Above this is the fuselage fuel tank and to the right of that is the firewall and in front of that the glycol header tank.

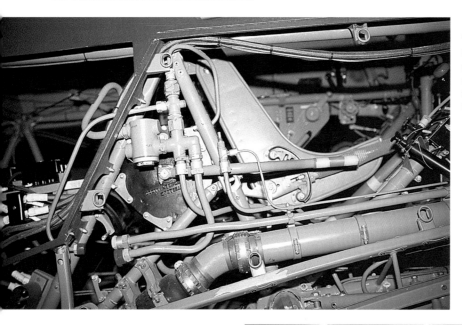

The access to equipment and systems in the Hurricane is excellent. Although not complete on this Hurricane, the pneumatic system is in place and the large coolant pipe is prominent.

The fuselage fuel tank sits above the pilot's feet. Although self-sealing, the tank could burn and many Hurricane pilots suffered horrific facial burns.

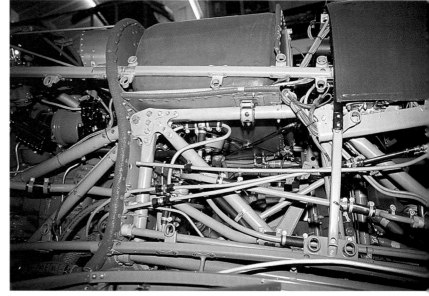

A high-level view of the front fuselage shows the fuselage fuel tank, firewall, coolant header tank and windscreen.

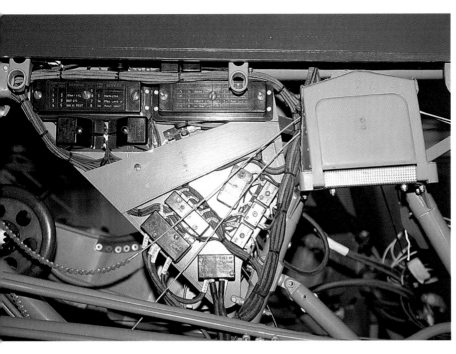

This view of the left-hand side of the fuselage shows the electrical junction boxes and the elevator trim wheel. This is operated by a chain around the wheel that is connected to the operating cables, which in this view are not connected to the trim and so are hanging loose.

BELOW: The front left-hand side of the fuselage showing the fuel tank and firewall.

ABOVE: The radio tray, behind the cockpit, is often not used on preserved Hurricanes, which are fitted with smaller, modern radios. This area is then very useful for storing the pilot's equipment. The circular fitting, bottom left, is the receptacle for the Dzus fastener.

The right side of the fuselage shows the first of the fairing panels being fitted. The handmade nature of the Hurricane means that these are unlikely to fit any other Hurricane and the registration of this one has been written on to the panel.

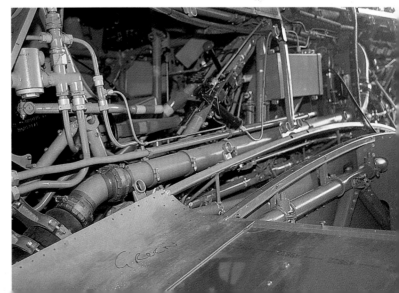

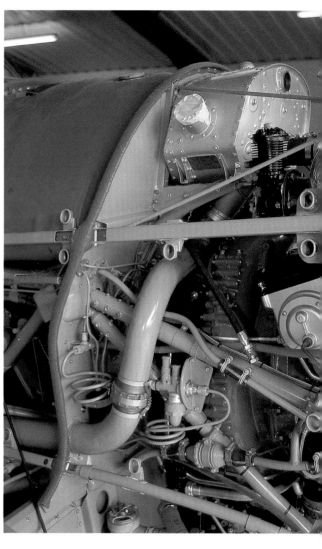

UPPER LEFT: The front fuselage showing the cowling panel frames. The oil tank, which forms the leading edge at the root on the port wing, is missing in this view and the oil pipes are plugged and wrapped for protection. The lower of these is the feed to the engine and the upper one the return from the oil cooler.

ABOVE: The glycol header tank is sealed with masking tape to stop debris entering during building. Also visible in this view are the stays that hold the firewall and engine cowling frames.

The under fuselage of the Hurricane has three downward identification lights roughly in line with the trailing edge of the wing. This view shows the metal panels and the under-fuselage stringers.

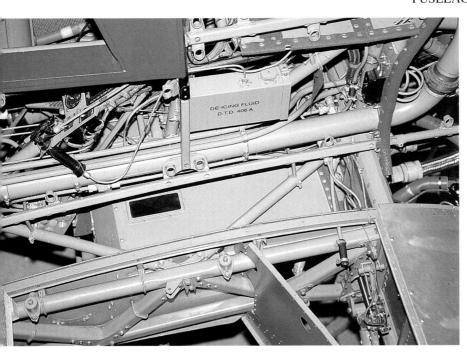

The wing root area showing the complexity of the structure and the amount of piping and wiring that has to be fitted.

The excellent access on the Hurricane is shown in this view of AE977. The cockpit area shows the air piping and the cockpit emergency access panel. This was not fitted to the prototype but was added to the production aircraft, as Service pilots would find it difficult to exit because of their flying clothing.

Undercarriage

The undercarriage on the Hurricane retracted inwards and the rear stay has to rotate around as well as move backwards for the wheel to clear the front spar. This view of the stay shows the sleeve that can slide along the bottom of the wing compression rib. Above is the join in the stay around which it rotates.

A close-up of the retraction jack.

ABOVE: The left hand oleo and wheel without the undercarriage fairings.

The rear of the wheel well.

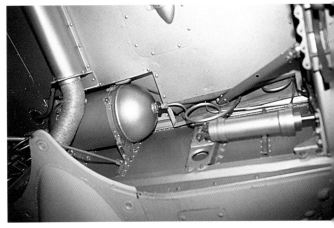

The emergency retraction air bottle is also housed in the wheel well.

ABOVE: The interior of the wheel well showing the retraction jack, hydraulic pipework and the upstop on the rib. To the upper left is a window in the wing upper surface that gives the pilot in the cockpit above a visual indication of the state of retraction.

ABOVE: The close-up of the complete gear on AE977. The brake pipe is just visible at the top of the leg, as is the housing for the rear stay.

A four-spoke wheel.

The outside of the Hurricane wheel, showing the axle fittings.

The inside of the complete undercarriage leg shows the brake pipe.

The outside of the undercarriage leg shows the six holes that house the bolts which fix the oleo to the straps that hold the door.

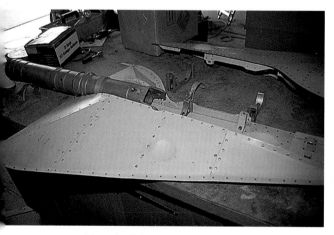

ABOVE: The wheel doors are wedge-shaped and are held in place by straps on to the oleo.

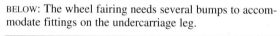

BELOW: The wheel fairing needs several bumps to accommodate fittings on the undercarriage leg.

ABOVE: The tailwheel on AE977 under load. Compare this with the one shown under construction (right).

BELOW: The tailwheel shown pivoted on the Shuttleworth Collection Sea Hurricane. Also visible in front is the cutout for the arrestor hook.

Engine

A beautifully restored Merlin III from a Battle of Britain Hurricane in the Spitfire and Hurricane Memorial museum at RAF Manston in Kent.

BELOW: A new engine mount at Hawker Restorations Ltd.

BELOW RIGHT: The underside of the engine shows the construction of the engine mount.

The engine installation on the Hurricane is surprisingly compact and benefits from the experience of the earlier Hart series of biplanes. The view from the cockpit was better than from many contemporary fighters, including the Spitfire.

A port side view of the engine. The missing section of leading edge that is formed by the oil tank is clearly visible.

The upper view of the engine. This is Packard-built Merlin 224.

ABOVE: The front view of the engine shows the reduction gear with one of the cylinder banks visible behind. The framing takes the front part of the cowling, and the two pipes that can be seen emerging through this are the hydraulic connections for the propeller variable pitch mechanism.

A close-up of the rear of the engine on the starboard side.

TOP: The Shuttleworth Sea Hurricane is fitted with a Merlin III, which is one of the oldest Merlin engines still flying.

ABOVE: The Merlin III has a starter magneto that can be rotated using a crank inserted into the starboard engine cowling. The chains turn the magneto, which provides a hotter spark to start the engine.

LEFT: A close-up of the starboard side of the engine showing the mount, firewall and oil connections. Also visible in this view are the leads to the spark plugs.

The fully installed engine in AE977. The upper cowling is in place, as much of the routine maintenance can be done with just the side panels removed.

The port side of AE977's engine.

AE977 was fitted with the early exhausts without the 'fishtails', as would have been the case on the Mark I it was meant to portray.

The exhausts on this partly completed Hurricane show no signs of the extreme heat that has affected those on AE977 after only a few hours' engine running.

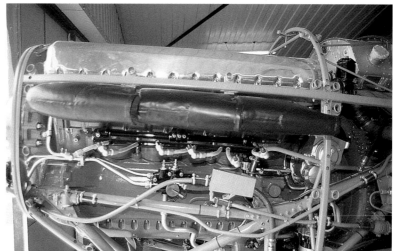

ABOVE: Starboard engine cowling ready for fitting.

BELOW: Hurricane exhausts in store at Hawker Engineering.The two connections to the cylinder exhaust ports are at the top with the exit at lower right.

This rear view of the exhausts clearly shows the openings.

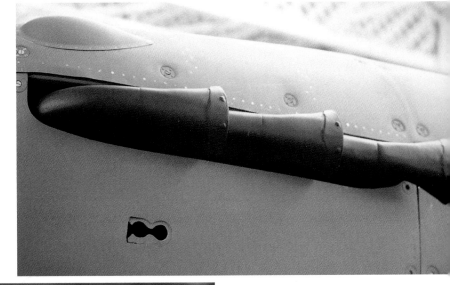

The Imperial War Museum Hurricane is painted as a Battle of Britain example although it is an ex-Russian machine. It is fitted with the 'fishtail' type of exhaust.

Fitted to the rear of the cylinder head on some Merlins was an air compressor for keeping the pneumatic system charged. Also visible is the fabric strip that stopped the engine cowlings from vibrating. The later style exhaust is also visible here.

Armament

Few preserved Hurricanes have their original armament. This RAF Museum Mark IA, P2617, has all eight machine guns in place and this view shows the aircraft serial marked on the ammunition boxes. (Chris Michell)

The access panel for the ammunition boxes was fastened at the front only and slotted into the structure at the rear for quick removal. (Chris Michell)

The guns are staggered so that the ammunition feeds do not conflict. (Chris Michell)

The barrels of the eight Brownings are fed into tubes and through the front spar. The electrical firing mechanism on the two forward guns is clearly visible. (Chris Michell)

This overall view of the gun bay shows the ammunition feeds, spent cartridge feeds and the wiring for the gun firing mechanism. (Chris Michell)

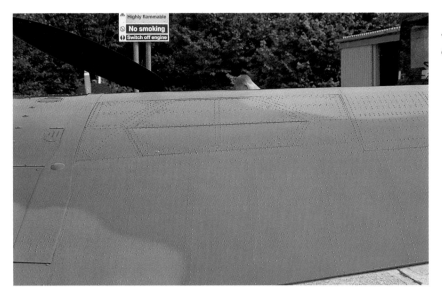

The access panels for the eight-machine-gun wing.

The underside of P2617's main gun cover panel shows good signs of wear. This Hurricane served during the Battle of France with 607 Squadron but missed the Battle of Britain as it was undergoing repairs following an accident on 29 May 1940. (Chris Michell)

The machine gun ejector ports under the port wing of the early, fabric wing, Mark I in the Science Museum in London. Just visible running across the wing from upper right to lower centre is the join in the fabric, which was applied at 45 degrees to the wing.

The fabric cover over the gunports was to stop freezing air rushing through the guns and freezing the mechanism. This would be penetrated by the first bullets, but the guns would then keep warm through use! This preserved aircraft has a metal cover in place of the fabric original.

The two extra gun ports for the twelve-gun wing are located outside the landing light position.

Preserved Hurricane IICs that have retained their cannons are even rarer than machine-gun Hurricanes, but this view shows the barrels on the Manston example. The fabric ends and the bear are, of course, non-original!

The barrel is supported by a massive casting attached to the front spar.

RIGHT: The Spitfire and Hurricane Memorial museum at Manston has an example of the 20mm cannon (centre) lying next to the Hurricane.

BELOW: A close-up of the ammunition drum and breech for the 20mm Hispano cannon.

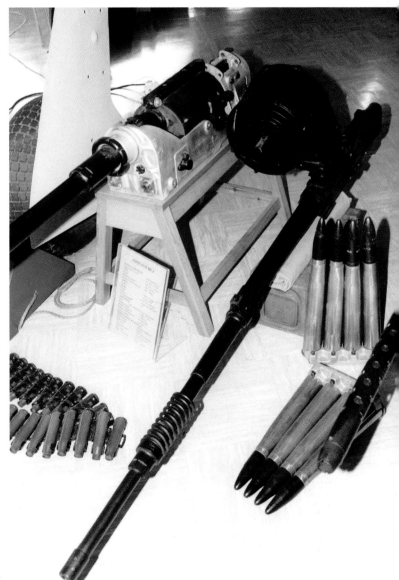

The access panels on the Hurricane IIC are very different to the machine-gun Hurricanes, as the weapons are much larger.

The ejector chutes for the cannon are much further back on the wing due to the length of the cannon. This view also shows the extended flaps.

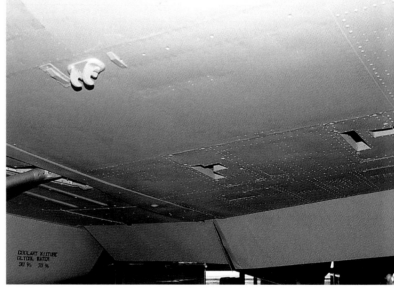

The Hispano cannon is fitted with a large recoil spring along the barrel.

Cockpit

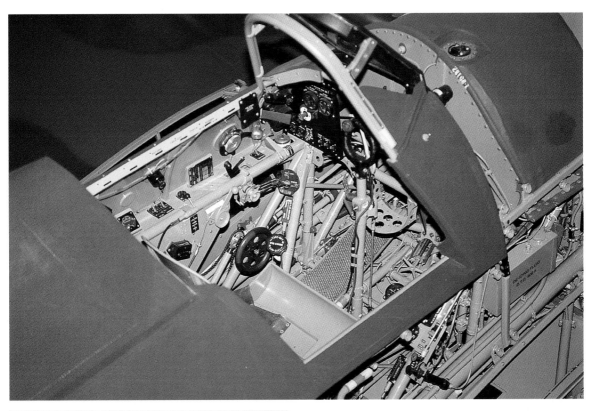

ABOVE: The overall view of a partly completed Hurricane shows the complexity of structure in the cockpit.

LEFT: The plywood of the doghouse provides the backrest for the pilot.

BELOW: Often mistaken for a door, the starboard break-out panel is for emergency use only. This view shows it removed for access to the cockpit during assembly and the shape of the area behind the pilot's head.

OPPOSITE PAGE, TOP: The overall view of the cockpit. This example has no gunsight fitted and a tray to take modern radios has been added behind where this will eventually be fitted.

OPPOSITE PAGE, BOTTOM: A view of the control column that gives a good impression of its position in relation to the panel. The metal handle in the centre of the handgrip is the brake lever that works in conjunction with the rudder pedals. When one pedal is pressed the brake will only work on that side and when the pedals are together the brakes work on both wheels. This was standard on many WWII and later RAF aircraft.

RIGHT: In common with many other RAF fighters of the period, the Hurricane control column moves forwards and backwards, but only the top part moves sideways. The movement is transferred through the cog seen at the rear of the column and down the cables that are attached. Also visible are the rudder pedals, the star-shaped adjuster between them and the pneumatic gauge.

BELOW: A general view of the seat and surrounding structure.

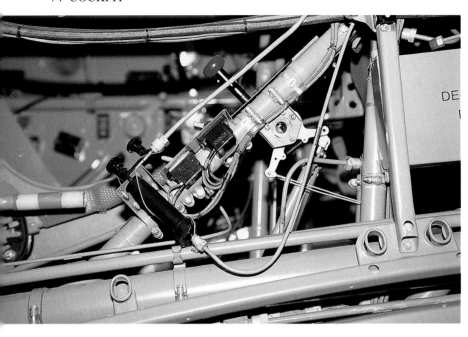

The undercarriage and flap controls viewed from the side, with the access panel removed.

The area around the pilot's feet is a little cluttered. The pedals are visible here, as is the star-shaped adjuster that allows the pedals to be moved backwards or forwards. The gauge between the pedals is for pneumatic pressure.

The inside of the emergency exit door with its release handle. Also attached is a map box.

Beneath the emergency exit door is the undercarriage control, with the flap position indicator and pressure gauge. Next to the seat is the seat height adjustment lever.

Looking down the right side of the seat. Any items dropped by the pilot end up in the depths of the fuselage.

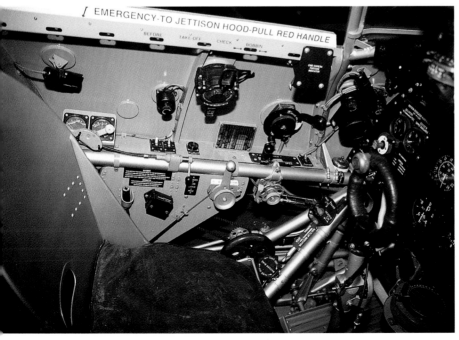

The left side of the cockpit. Of note are the plywood mounting plates behind many of the items fitted to the plywood 'doghouse'. Without these the cockpit walls would be too thin to take the fasteners.

ABOVE: The left-hand side of the panel.

ABOVE RIGHT: The left side of the cockpit.

The pivot on the control column. As the handle moves from side to side, the motion moves a cog onto which a short piece of chain is fitted. This in turn moves pushrods that extend down the sides of the control column which attach to bellcranks to operate the aileron cables. Visible at the top of the column is the chain guard and running down the back is the brake cable. Also visible in this photograph are the rudder pedals which have two positions for the feet. Raising the feet gives slightly better 'G' tolerance and a choice of position that is more comfortable on longer flights. The extensions at the top of the pedals will take leather straps as foot restraints.

ABOVE LEFT: The right-hand side of the panel, showing the compass between the pilot's knees, the basic RAF Blind Flying Panel on its rubber shock mountings in the centre of the panel and to the right of these are the engine instruments. Below these is the Ki-gas primer, and beneath that the flap control.

ABOVE: Close-up of undercarriage and flap controls.

Left side of the instrument panel. Centre bottom is the fuel cock and the panel to the left of the standard RAF Blind Flying Panel houses the oxygen instruments and magneto switches.

ABOVE LEFT: The Gyro gunsight is often not fitted to preserved flying Hurricanes as it can restrict forward view.

ABOVE: The windscreen and rear-view mirror on AE977.

The pilot's headrest on AE977. Also visible are the handle on the right-hand side and the cable running to the hood locking mechanism.

As pilot Stuart Goldspink prepares for engine start he has placed his gloves on the inside of the windscreen. Also visible is the armoured windscreen and the rear-view mirror.

A good view of the relative positions of cockpit windscreen, gun sight and rear-view mirror on the Shuttleworth Collection Sea Hurricane.

The canopy showing the various handles.

Hurricane Details

With many of the restoration team looking on, AE977 is started for an early test flight.

The Shuttleworth Sea Hurricane was built as a Hurricane Mark I and coverted into a Sea Hurricane for use on CAM ships. It is now flown regularly and is seen here undergoing some routine maintenence in the open at Old Warden.

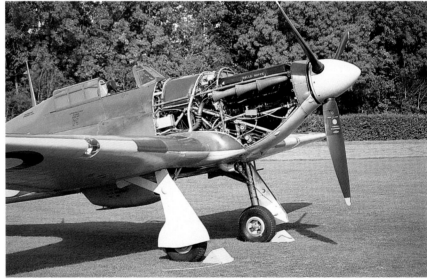

The Manston Hurricane spent many years on the gate of RAF Bentley Priory, where Fighter Command had its wartime headquarters. It was restored by members of the Medway branch of the Royal Aeronautical Society, and is now housed in a purpose-built memorial building alongside Spitfire XVI TB752.

Propeller stencilling.

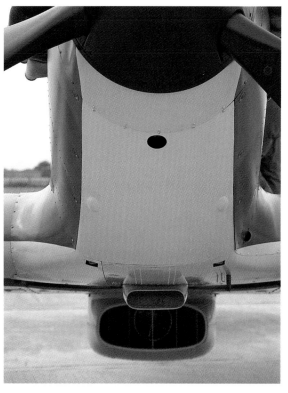

This head-on view of the nose shows the relative positions of the air intake, radiator bath and wing to fuselage fairings. The camera gun port is visible in the port wing root.

The Rotol propeller on the Sea Hurricane.

ABOVE: The underside of the nose showing the two jacking points and the carburettor air intake. The two tubes sticking down from the cowling are to drain excess oil.

A side view of AE977's nose. The early de Havilland spinner is of note.

The Manston Hurricane has the longer spinner of the Rotol propellor with the raised oil deflector behind.

The left side of AE977's nose. The bulges over the foremost exhaust port are to give clearance for the rocker covers.

Looking over the cockpit to the nose shows how much view it blocks when the aeroplane is on the ground although this is much less than the Spitfire.

LEFT: The wing root area showing the leading edge oil tank filler cap.

ABOVE: The air intake on the Sea Hurricane is fitted with a mesh guard to stop ingestion of debris.

ABOVE RIGHT: Close-up of the air intake and cowling oil drains.

The carburettor air intake on the Mark IIC is slightly larger than on the earlier marks.

The fuel filler for the wing tanks is found under a metal plate.

The fuel vent pipes are led out of the trailing edge under the strap that covers the centre section to outer wing join.

The power line from a trolley accumulator is attached to the fuselage plug on the right wing root. Also visible here is the non-slip area, very useful for RAF-issue boots on muddy airfields.

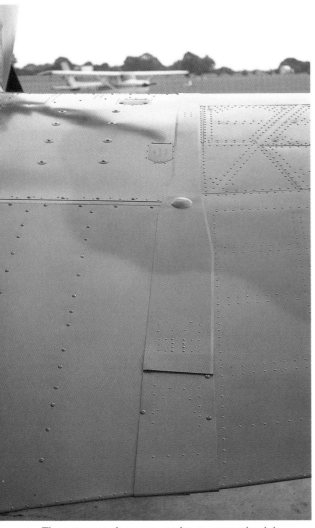

The strap over the centre section to outer wing join.

The wing to centre section join on L1592.

With L1592 suspended from the roof of the Science Museum, the position of the undercarriage doors with the wheels retracted can be seen.

The extended flaps on the Manston Hurricane.

ABOVE: The pitot head under the port wing.

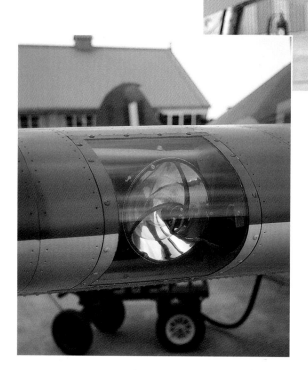

LEFT: The landing light in the starboard wing.

The front of the radiator shows the shape of the opening, with the oil cooler clearly visible in the centre. Of interest is the vertical stay in the centre of the opening and the pipes that are visible above the radiator in the undercarriage bay.

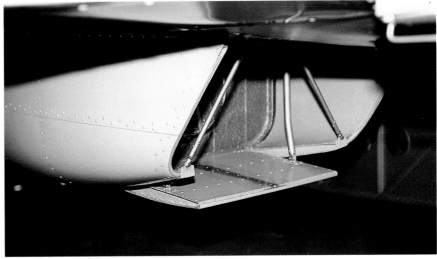

The rear view of the radiator from the port side shows the flap actuating rod and the oil cooler matrix.

This view of the underside shows the radiator flap and the stays at the rear of the radiator bath. Also visible are the downward indicator light panel, the clear transition between the metal-skinned areas and the fabric rear fuselage.

ABOVE: The aileron.

The wingtip to wing join.

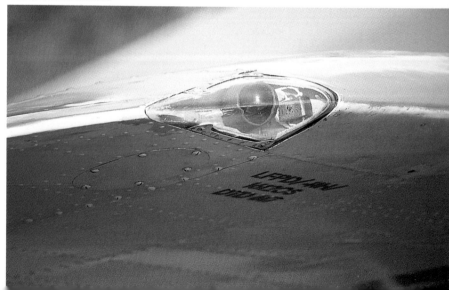

The wingtip navigation light.
The access panel is on the
underside.

The pilot's footstep in the extended position. When pulled out, this automatically opens the handhold in the fuselage.

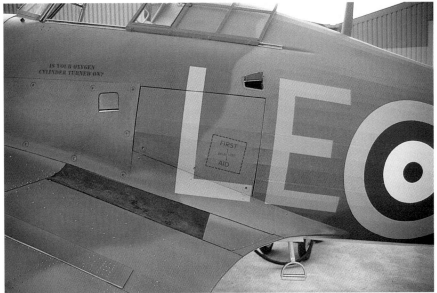

The open handhold is seen in this view, along with the kick-in footstep next to the cockpit. On the wing root is a non-slip panel.

The starboard-side access panels and non-slip walkway.

ABOVE LEFT: The Shuttleworth Collection takes great pride in fitting as much original equipment as possible, so its Hurricane is fitted with the early style aerial that mounts to the top of the fin.

ABOVE: The aerial mast on the Sea Hurricane.

LEFT: The radio mast as fitted to AE977.

BELOW LEFT: The static port for the Venturi-driven instruments is positioned along the fuselage.

BELOW: The radio mast on later Hurricanes remained the same despite not needing the long aerial between the fin and mast.

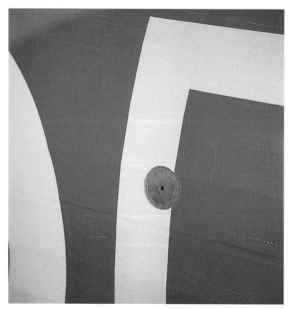

LEFT: Next to the radiator on a Sea Hurricane were catapult spools. This Hurricane was allocated to a CAM ship and could well have ended its life being ditched.

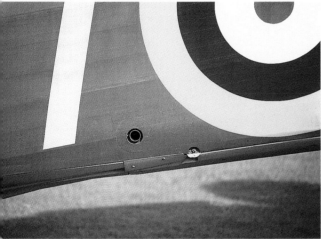

pivot point for the arrester hook is just in front of the jacking point.

A close-up of the catapult spool.

arrester hook on the Sea Hurricane was a simple 'A' frame attached lower longerons and retracted back to lie against the underside of selage. The ventral fairing had to be cut back to allow this.

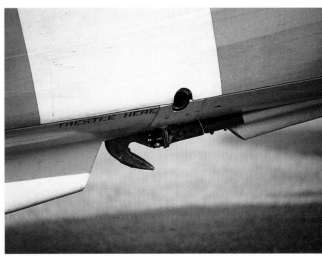

The catch to hold the arrester hook in place is fitted to the crosspiece that runs across above the jacking position.

LEFT AND BELOW: The back contours of the Hurricane form a gentle curve as they approach the fin.

ABOVE LEFT: The rear fuselage showing the jacking point and the squadron codes painted over the serial.

The fin to fuselage fairing.

ABOVE: The Hurricane tail at rest with fully deflected controls.

ABOVE LEFT: The leading edge of the elevator.

LEFT: With the elevator lowered the gap is much greater.

BELOW LEFT: The elevator trim tab.

BELOW: The underside of the tailplane showing the elevator in the partial up position and the tail to fuselage fairing.

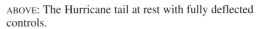

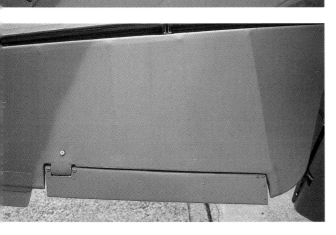

LEFT: The end of the tailplane showing the shape of the elevator balances.

An upper view of the elevator horn. Also visible is the cap strip for the tail fabric showing through its covering tape.

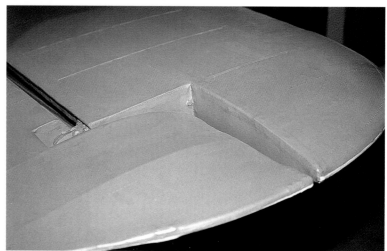

BELOW LEFT: The fin to tailplane join on AE977 showing the trim tab actuator, rudder cables and fairings.

BELOW: The rudder cables emerge from the fuselage underneath the tailplane. Visible here is the transition from fuselage fabric to metal covering around the tailplane and on the sternpost.

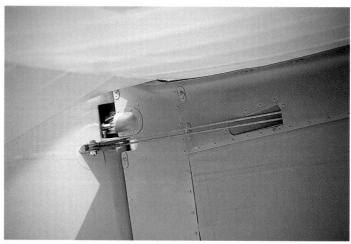

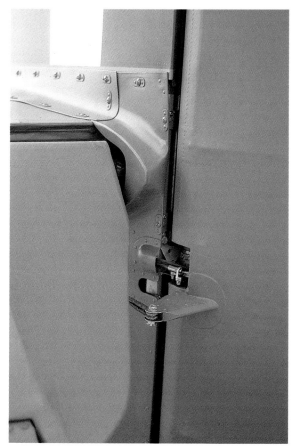

The rudder hinge and actuating horn.

The rudder trim tab actuator.

The rudder trim tab has its own mass balance.

A close-up of the rear identification light.

Tailpiece

AE977, the subject of many of the photographs in this book, is shown (above) being readied for an early test flight. This Hurricane was the second to be rebuilt at Hawker Engineering and its second first flight was in early 2000 after some 45,000 man hours of work. It can also be seen (below) second from the camera in this line of Sea Hurricanes. Of note is the early, blunt, Rotol spinner on the nearest Sea Hurricane and the de Havilland on AE977. (Crown Copyright)